MILAN

TRAVEL GUIDE 2024 AND BEYOND

Explore Culture, Hidden Gems, Cuisine, Exquisite Arts and Local Secrets in the Heart of the Po Basin, Northern Italy – Packed with Detailed Maps & Itinerary Planner

BY

JAMES W. PATRICK

Copyright © 2024 by James W. Patrick. All rights reserved. The content of this work, including but not limited to text, images, and other media, is owned by James W. Patrick and is protected under copyright laws and international agreements. No part of this work may be reproduced, shared, or transmitted in any form or by any means without the explicit written consent of James W. Patrick. Unauthorized use, duplication, or distribution of this material may lead to legal action, including both civil and criminal penalties. For permission requests or further inquiries, please reach out to the author via the contact details provided in the book or on the author's official page.

TABLE OF CONTENTS

Copyright 1
My Experience in Milan 5
Milan FAQ 7
Why Visit Milan? 10
What to Expect from this Guide 12

CHAPTER 1. INTRODUCTION TO MILAN 15
1.1 Overview of Milan's History 15
1.2 Geography and Climate 17
1.3 Exploring Milan's Neighborhoods 18
1.4 Cultural Diversity and Local Customs 21
1.5 Best Times to Visit 23

CHAPTER 2. ACCOMMODATION OPTIONS 26
2.1 Luxury Hotels and Resorts 26
2.2 Boutique and Design Hotels 29
2.3 Budget-Friendly Accommodations 31
2.4 Bed and Breakfasts 34
2.5 Unique Stays: Apartments and Guesthouses 37

CHAPTER 3. TRANSPORTATION IN MILAN 41
3.1 Public Transport Networks 41
3.2 Taxis and Ride-Sharing Services 43
3.3 Renting a Car or Bike 46
3.4 Walking Tours and Guided Transportation 48
3.5 Accessibility Considerations for Travelers 50

CHAPTER 4. TOP ATTRACTIONS/HIDDEN GEMS 53
4.1 Iconic Landmarks: Duomo di Milano, Sforza Castle, etc. 53
4.2 Hidden Gems: Off-the-Beaten-Path Discoveries 56
4.3 Museums and Art Galleries 59
4.4 Parks and Green Spaces 61

4.5 Architectural Marvels and Modern Landmarks..65

CHAPTER 5 PRACTICAL INFORMATION AND TRAVEL RESOURCES..................69
  5.1 Maps and Navigation..69
  5.2 Essential Packing List..71
  5.3 Visa Requirements and Entry Procedures..74
  5.4 Safety Tips and Emergency Contacts...76
  5.5 Currency, Banking, Budgeting and Money Matters.....................................79
  5.6 Language, Communication and Useful Phrases..81
  5.7 Useful Websites, Mobile Apps and Online Resources................................83
  5.8 Visitor Centers and Tourist Assistance..85

CHAPTER 6. CULINARY DELIGHTS...88
  6.1 Traditional Milanese Cuisine...88
  6.2 Fine Dining Experiences...90
  6.3 Street Food and Markets..93
  6.4 Wine Bars and Aperitivo Culture...95
  6.5 Cooking Classes and Food Tours...97

CHAPTER 7. CULTURE AND HERITAGE..100
  7.1 Historical Landmarks and Monuments..100
  7.2 Art and Architecture..103
  7.3 Performing Arts and Cultural Events...107
  7.4 Religious Sites and Festivals..111
  7.5 Preservation of Cultural Heritage in Milan...114

CHAPTER 8. OUTDOOR ACTIVITIES AND ADVENTURES................................118
  8.1 City Parks and Urban Green Spaces..118
  8.2 Cycling Routes and Bike Tours...121
  8.3 Day Trips to Lakes Como and Maggiore...125
  8.4 Hiking in the Lombardy Region...129
  8.5 Sports Events and Activities...132
  8.6 Family and Kids Friendly Activities..134
  8.7 Activities for Solo Travelers..137

CHAPTER 9. SHOPPING IN MILAN 141
9.1 Fashion Districts and Luxury Boutiques 141
9.2 Vintage and Designer Thrift Stores 143
9.3 Artisanal Crafts and Souvenirs 145
9.4 Specialty Food Shops and Markets 148
9.5 Shopping Malls and Department Stores 150

CHAPTER 10. DAY TRIPS AND EXCURSIONS 153
10.1 Lake Como: Scenic Beauty and Villas 154
10.2 Bergamo: Medieval Town and Venetian Walls 156
10.3 Verona: Romantic City of Romeo and Juliet 158
10.4 Pavia: Historic University Town 160
10.5 Turin: Baroque Architecture and Museums 162

CHAPTER 11. ENTERTAINMENT AND NIGHTLIFE 165
11.1 Restaurants: Gastronomic Experiences 165
11.2 Bars and Pubs: Local Hangouts 167
11.3 Nightclubs and Live Music Venues 170
11.4 Cultural Events and Performances 172
11.5 Safety Tips for Enjoying Milan's Nightlife 175
Conclusion and Insider Tips for Visitors 178

MILAN TRAVEL PLANNER 181

MY EXPERIENCE IN MILAN

Just saying the name "Milan", conjures up images of high fashion, exquisite art, and delectable cuisine. But let me tell you something I discovered during my recent visit to this enchanting city, Milan is so much more than its reputation suggests. It's a city of hidden gems, where every cobblestone street holds a story, and every corner reveals a piece of its captivating history. As a veteran traveler and author, I've had the privilege of exploring countless destinations around the globe. Yet, Milan holds a special place in my heart. It's a city that seamlessly blends tradition with modernity, offering visitors a unique experience unlike any other.

My journey in Milan began with a stroll through its historic center, where towering cathedrals and grand palaces line the streets. The majestic Duomo di Milano, with its intricate façade adorned with spires and statues, left me in awe of the craftsmanship of centuries past. Climbing to the rooftop offered a breathtaking panoramic view of the city, a sight that will forever be etched in my memory. But Milan isn't just about its architectural marvels; it's a haven for art enthusiasts as well. The Pinacoteca di Brera houses a magnificent collection of Renaissance masterpieces, including works by the likes of Caravaggio and Raphael. Standing before these timeless paintings, I couldn't help but feel a sense of reverence for the artists who once walked the same streets I was treading.

Of course, no visit to Milan would be complete without indulging in its culinary delights. From quaint trattorias to Michelin-starred restaurants, the city offers a gastronomic adventure like no other. I savored every bite of authentic risotto alla milanese, delighting in its creamy texture and subtle saffron flavor. And let's not forget about the decadent pastries – a visit to Milan wouldn't be complete without sampling a freshly baked cannolo or a flaky sfogliatella.

But perhaps what struck me most about Milan was its vibrant energy and passion for life. From the bustling markets of Mercato di Porta Palazzo to the chic boutiques of

Quadrilatero della Moda, there's an undeniable sense of excitement that permeates the air. I found myself getting lost in the rhythm of the city, swept up in its infectious enthusiasm. Yet amid all the hustle and bustle, Milan still manages to retain a sense of tranquility and elegance. The serene beauty of Parco Sempione provided a welcome respite from the urban jungle, with its lush greenery and peaceful lakes. It's moments like these that remind you to slow down and savor the simple pleasures of life.

As I reflect on my time in Milan, I can't help but feel grateful for the experiences it has afforded me. From exploring its rich history to savoring its culinary delights, every moment spent in this city has been nothing short of magical. And while words can paint a vivid picture, there's truly no substitute for experiencing it firsthand. So, to all my fellow travelers out there, I urge you to add Milan to your bucket list. Let its timeless elegance and vibrant culture captivate your heart and soul. Trust me, you won't regret it. Milan awaits, ready to enchant you with its charm and allure. Buon viaggio!

MILAN FAQ

1. What's the best time to visit Milan?

Milan is charming year-round, but spring (April to June) and fall (September to November) offer pleasant weather with fewer crowds. Avoid August when many locals go on vacation, and some businesses may be closed.

2. How do I get from Milan's airports to the city center?

Malpensa, Linate, and Bergamo are the main airports. Malpensa is connected by train, bus, and taxi. Linate is closer and accessible by bus or taxi. Bergamo is further away and connected by bus.

3. What are the must-visit attractions in Milan?

The Duomo di Milano, Leonardo da Vinci's Last Supper, Galleria Vittorio Emanuele II, Sforza Castle, and Brera Art Gallery are must-sees. Don't miss the fashion district and La Scala Opera House.

4. Is it necessary to book tickets in advance for attractions?

Yes, especially for popular attractions like the Last Supper and the Duomo's rooftop. Booking online ensures you secure your spot and avoids long queues.

5. What's the best way to get around Milan?

Milan has an efficient public transport system with metro, trams, and buses. Purchase a MilanoCard for unlimited travel or opt for single tickets if you're staying for a short period.

6. Where can I find the best shopping in Milan?

Head to Quadrilatero della Moda (Fashion Quadrilateral) for high-end designer boutiques. Corso Buenos Aires offers more affordable shopping, while Brera is perfect for unique boutiques and artisanal goods.

7. What should I eat in Milan?

Try risotto alla milanese, ossobuco, panettone, and gelato. Don't miss aperitivo, where you can enjoy drinks and complimentary snacks in the early evening.

8. Is tipping customary in Milan?

Tipping is not mandatory but appreciated for exceptional service. Round up the bill or leave 5-10% if service charge isn't included.

9. Are there any cultural etiquette I should be aware of?

Dress elegantly, especially if visiting religious sites or high-end establishments. Avoid discussing politics or religion unless initiated by locals.

10. Is It Safe To Walk Around Milan At Night?

Milan is generally safe, but it's best to stick to well-lit areas and avoid empty streets late at night. Exercise caution in crowded tourist areas to prevent pickpocketing.

11. What's the nightlife like in Milan?

Milan boasts a vibrant nightlife with trendy bars, clubs, and lounges. Navigli and Brera are popular areas for bar-hopping and live music.

12. How much Italian do I need to know to get by?

English is widely spoken, especially in tourist areas. Learning a few basic Italian phrases can enhance your experience and show respect for the local culture.

13. Are there any day trips I can take from Milan?

Yes, consider visiting Lake Como, Verona, or the picturesque towns of Cinque Terre for a day trip. They're easily accessible by train or bus.

14. What's the currency in Milan? Can I use credit cards?

The currency is the Euro (€). Credit cards are widely accepted, but it's advisable to carry some cash for small purchases and cafes.

15. What's the best way to experience Milan like a local?

Explore neighborhood markets, enjoy a leisurely meal at a family-run trattoria, and immerse yourself in the vibrant street art scene. Attend local events and festivals to truly experience Milan's authentic charm.

Milan is a city that seamlessly blends tradition with modernity, offering visitors a rich culture, history, and gastronomy. By addressing these FAQs, you'll be well-prepared to embark on a memorable journey through the heart of Italy. So pack your bags, immerse yourself in Milan's charm, and get ready for an unforgettable adventure! Buon viaggio!

WHY VISIT MILAN?

Milan entices travelers with its intricate blend of history, culture, and sophistication.. Steeped in centuries of tradition, this vibrant city is a testament to the enduring spirit of Italian artistry and innovation. From the majestic Duomo di Milano to the world-renowned masterpieces housed within its museums and galleries, Milan offers a captivating journey through time.

The Architectural Marvels
One cannot help but be mesmerized by the architectural splendor of Milan. The imposing presence of the Duomo, with its intricate façade and soaring spires, leaves visitors in awe of the craftsmanship of generations past. As you wander through the city streets, you'll encounter grand palaces, majestic cathedrals, and hidden courtyards, each telling a story of Milan's illustrious past. The sleek lines of modern skyscrapers stand in striking contrast to the historic landmarks, showcasing Milan's ability to seamlessly blend tradition with innovation.

A Haven for Art Enthusiasts
For art aficionados, Milan is a veritable paradise. The city's museums and galleries boast an impressive collection of masterpieces, ranging from Renaissance classics to contemporary works of art. The Pinacoteca di Brera houses iconic paintings by Caravaggio, Raphael, and Mantegna, while Leonardo da Vinci's Last Supper draws visitors from around the world with its haunting beauty. Every brushstroke tells a story, inviting visitors to delve deeper into the rich tapestry of Milan's artistic heritage.

A Culinary Delight
No trip to Milan is truly complete without savoring its culinary treasures. The city's vibrant food scene offers a feast for the senses, with tantalizing flavors and aromas waiting to be discovered around every corner. From creamy risotto alla milanese to decadent panettone, Milan's cuisine is a celebration of Italy's culinary heritage. Don't

miss the chance to sip an espresso at a cozy café or indulge in a leisurely aperitivo as the sun sets over the city skyline.

Fashion Capital of the World
Renowned as the fashion capital of the world, Milan is a paradise for fashionistas and trendsetters alike. The Quadrilatero della Moda, or Fashion Quadrilateral, is home to some of the most prestigious designer boutiques and luxury fashion houses, where haute couture meets cutting-edge style. Whether you're window shopping along Via Montenapoleone or attending a runway show during Milan Fashion Week, the city's sartorial prowess is impossible to ignore.

Vibrant Energy and Lifestyle
Beyond its architectural splendor and artistic treasures, Milan pulsates with a vibrant energy and zest for life. The city's bustling markets, lively piazzas, and chic cafes are a testament to the passion and creativity of its inhabitants. From the trendy neighborhoods of Brera and Navigli to the historic district of Porta Ticinese, Milan offers endless opportunities for exploration and discovery. Embrace the rhythm of the city, immerse yourself in its vibrant street life, and let Milan captivate your heart and soul.

Milan is a city that captivates the imagination and inspires the soul. Whether you're drawn to its rich history, artistic treasures, culinary delights, or fashion-forward flair, there's something for everyone to discover in this enchanting metropolis. So pack your bags, immerse yourself in Milan's timeless elegance, and prepare to embark on a journey of discovery that will leave you spellbound. Milan awaits, ready to enchant you with its charm and allure. Buon viaggio!

WHAT TO EXPECT FROM THIS GUIDE

Welcome to Milan, a city of unparalleled beauty, culture, and sophistication. As an author of numerous travel guides, I am thrilled to present to you this comprehensive guide, designed to help you make the most of your visit to this enchanting metropolis.

Navigating Milan: Maps and Navigation

Navigating Milan can be a breeze with the right tools at your disposal. Our guide includes detailed maps of the city center, public transportation routes, and key landmarks to ensure you never lose your way. Whether you're exploring the historic streets of Brera or navigating the bustling fashion district, our maps will be your trusty companions throughout your journey.

Accommodation Options: Where to Stay in Milan

Milan offers a diverse range of accommodation options to suit every budget and preference. From luxurious five-star hotels to charming boutique guesthouses, there's something for everyone. Our guide provides comprehensive reviews and recommendations, ensuring you find the perfect place to rest your head after a day of exploration.

Transportation: Getting Around Milan

Getting around Milan is a breeze thanks to its efficient public transportation system. Our guide covers everything you need to know about navigating the city by metro, tram, and bus, including ticketing information and travel tips. For those who prefer to explore on foot, we also highlight the city's pedestrian-friendly areas and scenic walking routes.

Top Attractions: Must-See Sights in Milan

Milan is home to a wealth of top attractions, from iconic landmarks to hidden gems waiting to be discovered. Our guide features in-depth profiles of must-visit sights such as the Duomo di Milano, Leonardo da Vinci's Last Supper, and the Galleria Vittorio

Emanuele II. Whether you're a history buff, art enthusiast, or fashion aficionado, Milan has something to offer everyone.

Practical Information and Travel Resources

Our comprehensive guide covers all the practical information you need to know before embarking on your Milan adventure. From visa requirements and currency exchange to safety tips and emergency contacts, we've got you covered. We also provide valuable resources such as recommended travel apps, language tips, and insider advice from seasoned travelers.

Culinary Delights: Sampling Milan's Gastronomic Treasures

No trip to Milan is truly complete without indulging in its world-class cuisine. Our guide takes you on a culinary journey through the city's vibrant food scene. from traditional trattorias serving up hearty pasta dishes to chic cafes offering innovative fusion cuisine. We also highlight must-try delicacies such as risotto alla milanese, panettone, and gelato, ensuring you experience the true flavors of Milan.

Culture and Heritage: Immersing Yourself in Milan's Rich Heritage

Milan is steeped in history and culture, with a wealth of museums, galleries, and historic sites waiting to be explored. Our guide delves into the city's rich heritage, uncovering hidden gems and lesser-known attractions that offer a glimpse into Milan's storied past. Whether you're marveling at Renaissance masterpieces or wandering through ancient ruins, Milan's cultural treasures are sure to leave a lasting impression.

Outdoor Activities and Adventures: Exploring Milan's Natural Beauty

While Milan may be known for its urban sophistication, it also boasts an abundance of outdoor activities and adventures for nature lovers. Our guide highlights scenic parks, gardens, and green spaces where you can escape the hustle and bustle of the city and reconnect with nature. Whether you're cycling along the Navigli canals or picnicking in Parco Sempione, Milan offers plenty of opportunities for outdoor exploration.

Shopping: Indulging in Retail Therapy in Milan's Fashion District

Milan is synonymous with high fashion, and no visit would be complete without indulging in a spot of retail therapy. Our guide showcases the city's premier shopping destinations, from the exclusive boutiques of the Quadrilatero della Moda to the bustling street markets of Porta Ticinese. Whether you're in search of designer labels or unique artisanal goods, Milan offers endless opportunities for shopping enthusiasts.

Day Trips and Excursions: Exploring Beyond Milan's Borders

While Milan has plenty to offer, its strategic location also makes it the perfect base for day trips and excursions to nearby attractions. Our guide highlights popular day trip destinations such as Lake Como, Verona, and the Cinque Terre, providing all the information you need to plan your adventure. Whether you're craving a scenic getaway or a cultural excursion, Milan's proximity to other iconic destinations makes it the ideal starting point for exploration.

Entertainment and Nightlife: Embracing Milan's Vibrant Night Scene

When the sun sets, Milan comes alive with a vibrant nightlife scene that caters to every taste and preference. Our guide features recommendations for the best bars, clubs, and live music venues where you can dance the night away and mingle with locals and fellow travelers alike. Whether you're sipping cocktails in a chic rooftop bar or catching a live performance at La Scala Opera House, Milan offers endless opportunities for entertainment and excitement after dark. Milan is a city of endless possibilities, where history, culture, and modernity converge to create an unforgettable experience. With this comprehensive guide as your companion, you'll be well-equipped to explore all that this enchanting metropolis has to offer. So pack your bags, prepare to be enchanted, and embark on a journey of discovery through the heart of Italy. Milan awaits, ready to captivate your imagination and leave you longing for more. Buon viaggio!

CHAPTER 1
INTRODUCTION TO MILAN

1.1 Overview of Milan's History

This bustling metropolis is a treasure trove of history, a place where each corner whispers tales of centuries past. Join me on a journey through Milan's storied past, as we uncover the secrets of this captivating city. Milan's history dates back over two millennia, with origins rooted in the Celtic settlement of Mediolanum. Nestled in the fertile plains of Northern Italy, Mediolanum flourished under Roman rule, becoming a bustling hub of commerce and culture. The city's strategic location made it a vital center of trade, connecting the Roman Empire to the rest of Europe.

The fall of the Roman Empire heralded a new era for Milan, as it fell under the rule of various conquerors, including the Byzantines, Lombards, and Franks. Each successive dynasty left its mark on the city, shaping its architecture, culture, and identity. It wasn't until the Renaissance that Milan experienced a resurgence, emerging as a beacon of art, literature, and innovation. One of Milan's most iconic landmarks, the magnificent Duomo di Milano, stands as a testament to the city's enduring legacy. This Gothic masterpiece took over six centuries to complete, with construction beginning in 1386. Its intricate facade, adorned with countless statues and spires, is a testament to the skill and craftsmanship of generations past. Climbing to the rooftop offers a panoramic view of the city, a breathtaking vista that leaves visitors in awe of Milan's timeless beauty.

Another highlight of Milan's historical landscape is the imposing Sforza Castle, located in the heart of the city. Built in the 15th century by the ruling Sforza dynasty, the castle served as a symbol of power and prestige Presently, it hosts numerous museums and art institutions, exhibiting Milan's abundant cultural legacy. No exploration of Milan's history would be complete without a visit to Leonardo da Vinci's Last Supper. Located in the refectory of the Convent of Santa Maria delle Grazie, this iconic fresco is a masterpiece of Renaissance art. Painted between 1495 and 1498, it depicts the moment when Jesus announces that one of his disciples will betray him. The fresco's exquisite detail and emotional depth make it a must-see for art enthusiasts and history buffs alike.

But Milan's history isn't confined to its grand landmarks and famous artworks. It's woven into the fabric of everyday life, evident in the charming neighborhoods, bustling markets, and lively piazzas that dot the cityscape. From the bohemian district of Brera to the vibrant Navigli canals, each corner of Milan offers a glimpse into its rich tapestry of history and culture. Milan is more than just a city—it's a living, breathing testament to the resilience and creativity of the human spirit. Its history is a tapestry woven from the threads of countless civilizations, each contributing to the vibrant mosaic that defines Milan today. So come, immerse yourself in the beauty and majesty of Milan's past, and let its rich history ignite your imagination and curiosity. The journey awaits.

1.2 Geography and Climate

Milan is nestled in the heart of the Po River Valley. Surrounded by the Alpine foothills to the north and the Apennine Mountains to the south, Milan enjoys a picturesque setting that is both awe-inspiring and geographically diverse. The city's strategic location has made it a hub of commerce, culture, and innovation for centuries, with its landscape shaping its identity and character.

Understanding Milan's Climate

AMilan experiences a humid subtropical climate, characterized by hot summers and cold, damp winters. However, its proximity to the Alps and the Po Valley moderates extreme temperatures, creating a relatively temperate climate year-round. Indeed, Milan experiences four distinct seasons throughout the year, each bestowing its own unique charm and allure upon visitors.

Spring: March to May

Spring in Milan heralds the awakening of nature, with blooming flowers and mild temperatures creating an inviting atmosphere for outdoor exploration. Average temperatures range from 10°C (50°F) to 20°C (68°F), making it an ideal time to wander through Milan's charming neighborhoods, visit its historic landmarks, and indulge in al fresco dining at sidewalk cafes. However, occasional showers are common, so it's advisable to pack an umbrella and light layers.

Summer: June to August

Summer in Milan brings long, sunny days and warm temperatures, with average highs ranging from 25°C (77°F) to 30°C (86°F). The city comes alive with outdoor festivals, concerts, and cultural events, drawing visitors from around the world to bask in its vibrant energy. While the weather is generally pleasant, occasional heatwaves can occur, so be sure to stay hydrated and seek shade when necessary.

Autumn: September to November

Autumn in Milan is a feast for the senses, with crisp air, golden foliage, and cooler temperatures setting the stage for a memorable visit. Average temperatures range from 15°C (59°F) to 20°C (68°F), making it an ideal time for sightseeing, exploring Milan's parks and gardens, and savoring seasonal delicacies at local trattorias. It's also the season for fashion enthusiasts, as Milan Fashion Week takes center stage, showcasing the latest trends and designs.

Winter: December to February

Winter in Milan is characterized by chilly temperatures and occasional snowfall, creating a picturesque backdrop for holiday festivities and cultural celebrations. Average temperatures range from 0°C (32°F) to 10°C (50°F), with colder temperatures experienced in the evenings. While the city may not be as crowded as during the peak tourist season, it offers a cozy atmosphere and plenty of opportunities to explore its indoor attractions, such as museums, galleries, and theaters.

Navigating Milan's Geography

Navigating Milan's geography is relatively straightforward, thanks to its well-developed transportation network and compact city center. The city is divided into nine administrative zones, with the historic center located in Zone 1. Milan's efficient public transport system, including metro, trams, and buses, makes it easy to explore its diverse neighborhoods and attractions. Additionally, the city is pedestrian-friendly, with many of its major landmarks and shopping districts within walking distance of each other. Milan's geography and climate offer a captivating backdrop for exploration and discovery. Whether you're wandering through its historic streets, soaking up the sun in its picturesque parks, or immersing yourself in its vibrant cultural scene, Milan welcomes visitors with open arms, inviting them to experience its beauty and charm in every season. So pack your bags, prepare for adventure, and embark on a journey through Milan's diverse landscape and dynamic climate. The city awaits, ready to enchant you with its wonders.

1.3 Exploring Milan's Neighborhoods

Milan, a city steeped in history and brimming with culture, invites travelers to explore its vibrant neighborhoods, each offering a unique glimpse into the soul of the city. As a seasoned traveler and author, I've had the privilege of wandering through Milan's streets, immersing myself in its rich tapestry of life and discovering hidden gems around every corner. Join me as we uncover six diverse ways to explore Milan's neighborhoods, each promising an unforgettable experience.

Wander Through the Historic Center
The heart of Milan beats strongest in its historic center, where ancient monuments and modern marvels coexist in perfect harmony. Start your journey at the iconic Piazza del Duomo, home to the magnificent Duomo di Milano and the elegant Galleria Vittorio Emanuele II. From there, meander through the winding streets of the Brera district, where charming cafes, art galleries, and boutiques beckon you to linger a while. Don't miss the chance to explore the imposing Sforza Castle and stroll along the picturesque Navigli canals, where vibrant street markets and lively bars await.

Indulge in Fashion and Luxury
For fashion enthusiasts and trendsetters, Milan is a paradise unlike any other. Dive into the world of haute couture in the Quadrilatero della Moda, home to prestigious designer boutiques and flagship stores. Lose yourself in the opulent elegance of Via Montenapoleone, where luxury brands and high-end fashion houses line the streets. Take a moment to admire the sleek lines of the Armani Silos museum, dedicated to the legendary fashion designer Giorgio Armani, and immerse yourself in the timeless allure of Italian style.

Discover Bohemian Charm in Brera
Nestled in the heart of Milan, the Brera district exudes a bohemian charm that captivates the soul. Lose yourself in the labyrinthine streets of this historic neighborhood, where cobblestone alleys and hidden courtyards reveal a world of artistic inspiration. Explore the Pinacoteca di Brera, home to one of Italy's most prestigious art collections, and wander through the bustling Mercato di Via San Marco, where local

artisans showcase their craft. End your day with a leisurely meal at a quaint trattoria, savoring traditional Milanese dishes and soaking up the vibrant atmosphere.

Soak Up the Sun in Porta Nuova

Experience Milan's modern side in the sleek and sophisticated neighborhood of Porta Nuova. Marvel at the futuristic architecture of the Unicredit Tower and the Bosco Verticale, two iconic skyscrapers that dominate the skyline. Take a leisurely stroll through the lush greenery of the Giardini di Porta Nuova, a tranquil oasis in the heart of the city. Indulge in gourmet cuisine at one of the neighborhood's chic restaurants or sip cocktails at a trendy rooftop bar as the sun sets over the bustling city below.

Explore the Diversity of Chinatown

Immerse yourself in the vibrant colors and exotic flavors of Milan's Chinatown, a melting pot of cultures and cuisines. Start your adventure at the majestic Arch of Peace, then wander through the bustling streets of Via Paolo Sarpi, lined with traditional Chinese restaurants, tea shops, and markets. Discover hidden gems like the Guan Yin Temple, a serene Buddhist sanctuary tucked away amidst the hustle and bustle. Be sure to sample authentic Chinese delicacies and street food favorites, from steaming dumplings to savory baozi, as you embrace the vibrant energy of this dynamic neighborhood.

Experience Local Life in Navigli

Escape the tourist crowds and immerse yourself in the laid-back atmosphere of Navigli, Milan's beloved canal district. Follow the tranquil waters of the Naviglio Grande and the Naviglio Pavese as they wind their way through charming neighborhoods and picturesque squares. Explore artisan workshops and vintage shops, where you can uncover unique treasures and one-of-a-kind souvenirs. Relax at a waterfront cafe or bar, sipping an aperitivo as you watch the world go by. As the sun sets, join the locals for a leisurely passeggiata along the canal banks, soaking up the timeless charm of this beloved neighborhood. Milan's neighborhoods offer a myriad of experiences waiting to be discovered. Whether you're exploring the historic center, indulging in luxury fashion, or immersing yourself in local life, each neighborhood promises a unique glimpse into the soul of the city. So pack your bags, lace up your walking shoes, and embark on a journey through Milan's diverse landscapes and vibrant communities. The adventure awaits.

1.4 Cultural Diversity and Local Customs

As a veteran traveler and author, I've had the privilege of immersing myself in the cultural tapestry of countless destinations around the world. Yet, it's Milan's rich diversity and vibrant local customs that continue to captivate my heart. Join me as we delve into six unique cultural experiences that make Milan a city like no other.

A Culinary Journey Through Milan's Gastronomic Delights

Milan's culinary scene is a feast for the senses, reflecting the city's diverse cultural influences and rich gastronomic heritage. Start your culinary journey in the historic Brera district, where traditional Milanese trattorias serve up hearty dishes like ossobuco and risotto alla milanese. Venture into Chinatown to sample authentic Chinese cuisine, from steaming dim sum to savory noodle soups. Don't miss the chance to indulge in aperitivo, a beloved Milanese tradition where locals gather for pre-dinner drinks and complimentary snacks. Whether you're savoring gelato in a bustling piazza or dining al fresco along the Navigli with its charming canals and vibrant culinary scene, Milan offers a plethora of delightful gastronomic experiences that are sure to tantalize your taste buds and leave you craving more.

Embracing Milan's Artistic Legacy

Milan has long been a hub of artistic innovation and creativity, boasting a rich legacy of masterpieces that span centuries. Begin your artistic exploration at the iconic Pinacoteca di Brera, home to a world-class collection of Renaissance paintings by masters like Caravaggio and Raphael. Discover contemporary art at the Fondazione Prada, a cutting-edge cultural complex housed in a historic distillery. Explore the vibrant street art scene in the up-and-coming Isola district, where colorful murals and graffiti adorn the walls of abandoned buildings and urban alleyways. Whether you're admiring classical sculptures at the Castello Sforzesco or discovering avant-garde installations at the HangarBicocca, Milan's artistic landscape is sure to inspire and intrigue.

Celebrating Milan's Fashion Forward Spirit

Milan is synonymous with style and sophistication, serving as the epicenter of Italy's fashion industry and a global trendsetter in haute couture. Dive into the world of high fashion in the Quadrilatero della Moda, home to prestigious designer boutiques and flagship stores. Explore the historic Galleria Vittorio Emanuele II, a luxurious shopping arcade adorned with intricate mosaics and elegant storefronts. Discover emerging designers and independent labels in the trendy Brera and Navigli districts, where fashion-forward boutiques and concept stores abound. Whether you're attending a runway show during Milan Fashion Week or browsing the latest collections at a chic boutique, Milan's fashion scene promises an unforgettable experience for style enthusiasts and trendsetters alike.

Immersing Yourself in Milan's Music and Theater Scene

Milan is a city that pulses with the rhythm of music and the energy of live performance, offering a dynamic cultural landscape that spans classical opera to cutting-edge theater. Experience the grandeur of La Scala, one of the world's most renowned opera houses, where you can witness breathtaking performances in an atmosphere of elegance and sophistication houses, where legendary performances by Verdi, Puccini, and Rossini have captivated audiences for centuries. Discover contemporary theater and experimental performance art at venues like the Teatro degli Arcimboldi and the Piccolo Teatro di Milano. From classical concerts in historic churches to underground jazz clubs in the Navigli district, Milan's music and theater scene offers something for every taste and preference.

Exploring Milan's Religious Heritage

Milan is a city of faith, boasting a rich religious heritage that spans millennia and encompasses a diverse array of traditions and beliefs. Begin your spiritual journey at the majestic Duomo di Milano, a soaring Gothic cathedral adorned with intricate spires and statues. Explore the spiritual significance of iconic landmarks like the Basilica di Sant'Ambrogio, dedicated to the patron saint of Milan, and the Sanctuary of Santa Maria alla Fontana, home to a miraculous fresco of the Virgin Mary. Discover the multicultural character of Milan's religious landscape in neighborhoods like Little Jerusalem, where historic synagogues and kosher delis coexist alongside Roman Catholic churches and Islamic mosques. Whether you're attending mass at a centuries-old basilica or participating in a multicultural festival celebrating Milan's religious diversity, the city's spiritual heritage is sure to inspire and uplift.

Experiencing Milan's Festivals and Traditions
Milan is a city that loves to celebrate, with a calendar full of vibrant festivals and traditions that bring communities together in joyous revelry. Join the festivities during Carnevale Ambrosiano, Milan's own version of Carnival, where colorful parades, masked balls, and street performances take center stage. Experience the magic of Navigli Art Nights, an annual event where the canal district comes alive with art installations, live music, and cultural exhibitions. Celebrate Milan's culinary heritage during the Fiera di Sant'Ambrogio, a traditional market that honors the city's patron saint with food stalls, folk music, and festive parades.

Whether you're ringing in the New Year with fireworks in Piazza del Duomo or dancing the night away at a summer music festival in Parco Sempione, Milan's festive spirit is infectious and exhilaratin Milan's cultural diversity and local customs offer a captivating glimpse into the soul of this vibrant city. Whether you're indulging in culinary delights, immersing yourself in artistic innovation, or celebrating centuries-old traditions, Milan promises an unforgettable journey of discovery and delight. So pack your bags, embrace the spirit of adventure, and prepare to be swept away by the magic of Milan's cultural mosaic. The city awaits, ready to welcome you with open arms and open hearts.

1.5 Best Time to Visit
Milan, with its rich tapestry of history, culture, and charm, beckons travelers year-round. However, there are certain seasons that stand out as particularly ideal for experiencing the city at its best.

Spring: April to June

Springtime in Milan is a magical affair, as the city awakens from its winter slumber with blooming flowers, mild temperatures, and a sense of renewal in the air. From April to June, Milan comes alive with vibrant colors and bustling activity, making it an ideal time for sightseeing, outdoor exploration, and cultural experiences. The weather is pleasantly mild, with temperatures ranging from 10°C to 25°C (50°F to 77°F), making it perfect for leisurely strolls through the city's historic streets and charming neighborhoods.

Summer: July to September

Summer in Milan is a time of long, sunny days, al fresco dining, and outdoor festivals. From July to September, the city basks in warm temperatures, with average highs ranging from 25°C to 30°C (77°F to 86°F). While the weather can be hot and humid at times, it provides the perfect backdrop for exploring Milan's lush parks and gardens, indulging in gelato by the Duomo, and attending open-air concerts and cultural events. Summer also coincides with Milan Fashion Week in September, offering fashion enthusiasts the chance to witness the latest trends and designs firsthand.

Epic Events and Festivals in Milan

Milan is a city that loves to celebrate, with a calendar full of epic events and festivals that showcase its vibrant culture and heritage.

Milan Fashion Week

One of the most prestigious events on the global fashion calendar, Milan Fashion Week takes place twice a year in February/March and September/October. Fashion designers, models, celebrities, and industry insiders descend upon the city to showcase the latest collections and trends, turning Milan into a hotbed of style and creativity. Even if you're not directly involved in the fashion world, the energy and excitement of Milan Fashion Week are palpable throughout the city, with events, parties, and exhibitions happening at every turn.

Salone del Mobile

Every April, Milan becomes the epicenter of the design world with the Salone del Mobile, the largest and most prestigious furniture fair in the world. Designers, architects, and furniture manufacturers from around the globe gather to showcase their latest creations and innovations, transforming Milan into a hub of creativity and inspiration. Whether you're a design enthusiast or simply appreciate beautiful craftsmanship, the Salone del Mobile offers a unique opportunity to explore the cutting edge of design and immerse yourself in Milan's design culture.

Christmas Markets
During the holiday season, Milan comes alive with the festive spirit, as Christmas markets pop up throughout the city, filling the air with the scent of roasted chestnuts, mulled wine, and seasonal treats. From the iconic markets in Piazza Duomo and Piazza Castello to the charming markets in the Navigli district and Brera neighborhood, there's no shortage of holiday cheer to be found in Milan. Browse stalls selling handmade crafts, decorations, and gifts, sample traditional Christmas sweets, and soak up the magical atmosphere of the season.

Navigli Art Nights
One of the most anticipated events of the year, Navigli Art Nights takes place every June, transforming the city's historic canal district into a vibrant cultural playground. Galleries, studios, and cultural institutions open their doors late into the night, hosting exhibitions, performances, and installations showcasing the best of Milan's contemporary art scene.Wander through the bustling streets, explore hidden galleries, and immerse yourself in the creative energy of Navigli Art Nights, an event that showcases the vibrant art scene of Milan's Navigli district, an event that showcases the vibrant art scene of Milan's Navigli district an unforgettable celebration of Milan's artistic spirit. The best times to visit Milan are during the spring and summer months, when the city comes alive with vibrant colors, cultural events, and outdoor festivities.

Whether you're exploring Milan's historic landmarks, indulging in its culinary delights, or immersing yourself in its vibrant arts scene, there's no shortage of experiences to captivate and inspire you throughout the year. So pack your bags, plan your itinerary, and get ready to embark on an unforgettable journey through the heart of Milan. The city awaits, ready to welcome you with open arms and endless possibilities.

CHAPTER 2
ACCOMMODATION OPTIONS

Click the link or Scan QR Code with a device to view a comprehensive map of various Accommodation Options in Milan – https://shorturl.at/ptvNP

2.1 Luxury Hotels and Resorts

Milan, the epitome of style and sophistication, offers an array of luxurious hotels and resorts that cater to the discerning traveler seeking unparalleled comfort and elegance. From historic landmarks to modern marvels, these six establishments redefine luxury accommodation in the heart of Milan.

Hotel Principe di Savoia

Located in the prestigious Piazza della Repubblica, Hotel Principe di Savoia is a timeless icon of Milanese luxury. This elegant hotel exudes Old-World charm with its lavish interiors, impeccable service, and breathtaking views of the city skyline. Prices for lodging start at €400 per night for a classic room, with suites available from €1,000 per night. Amenities include a luxurious spa and wellness center, rooftop pool with panoramic views, and Michelin-starred dining at Acanto restaurant. Special services include personal butler service, limousine transfers, and exclusive access to VIP events. Prices for meals vary, with a gourmet breakfast buffet priced at €40 per person. For reservations and bookings, visit the official website at (www.dorchestercollection.com/en/milan/hotel-principe-di-savoia)

Mandarin Oriental Milan

Nestled in the heart of Milan's fashion district, Mandarin Oriental Milan offers a tranquil oasis of luxury and refinement. Prices for lodging start at €600 per night for a deluxe room, with suites available from €1,200 per night. Each room and suite is elegantly appointed with modern amenities and Italian-inspired decor. Guests can indulge in world-class dining at the hotel's Michelin-starred restaurant, Seta, or relax and unwind at the luxurious spa and wellness center. Special services include personalized concierge assistance, bespoke experiences, and exclusive access to fashion events and cultural attractions. Prices for meals range from €50 to €150 per person. For reservations and bookings, visit the official website at (www.mandarinoriental.com/milan)

Bulgari Hotel Milan

Situated in the upscale Brera district, Bulgari Hotel Milan exudes understated elegance and sophistication. Prices for lodging start at €500 per night for a superior room, with suites available from €1,200 per night. Each room and suite is tastefully decorated with contemporary Italian furnishings and state-of-the-art amenities. Guests can indulge in gourmet cuisine at the hotel's Michelin-starred restaurant, Il Ristorante, or unwind with a signature cocktail at the stylish bar. Special services include personalized shopping experiences, private dining options, and access to the hotel's private garden oasis. Prices for meals range from €50 to €200 per person. For reservations and bookings, visit the official website at (www.bulgarihotels.com/en_US/milan).

Excelsior Hotel Gallia, a Luxury Collection Hotel

Located adjacent to Milan Central Station, Excelsior Hotel Gallia is a modern masterpiece of luxury and sophistication. Prices for lodging start at €350 per night for a classic room, with suites available from €800 per night. Each room and suite boasts contemporary design, luxurious amenities, and panoramic views of the city skyline. Guests can dine at the hotel's Michelin-starred restaurant, Terrazza Gallia, or relax and unwind at the luxurious spa and wellness center. Special services include personalized concierge assistance, luxury car rentals, and access to exclusive events and experiences. Prices for meals range from €40 to €150 per person. For reservations and bookings, visit the official website at (www.marriott.com/hotels/travel/milgl-excelsior-hotel-gallia-a-luxury-collection-hotel-milan).

Park Hyatt Milan

Nestled in the heart of Milan's historic district, Park Hyatt Milan offers a luxurious retreat in the midst of the city's bustling streets. Prices for lodging start at €450 per night for a Park King room, with suites available from €1,000 per night. Each room and suite is elegantly appointed with contemporary furnishings, marble bathrooms, and luxurious amenities. Guests can dine at the hotel's Michelin-starred restaurant, VUN Andrea Aprea, or unwind with a cocktail at the stylish Mio Lab Bar. Special services include personalized concierge assistance, private dining options, and access to the hotel's spa and fitness center. Prices for meals range from €50 to €200 per person. For reservations and bookings, visit the official website at (www.hyatt.com/en-US/hotel/italy/park-hyatt-milan/milan)

Four Seasons Hotel Milano

Housed in a restored 15th-century convent, Four Seasons Hotel Milano seamlessly blends historic charm with modern luxury. Prices for lodging start at €500 per night for a deluxe room, with suites available from €1,200 per night. Each room and suite features elegant decor, luxurious amenities, and views of the hotel's tranquil courtyard or the city skyline. Guests can dine at the hotel's Michelin-starred restaurant, Il Teatro, or unwind with a cocktail at the stylish lobby bar. Special services include personalized shopping experiences, private guided tours, and access to the hotel's spa and wellness center. Prices for meals range from €50 to €200 per person. For reservations and bookings, visit: (www.fourseasons.com/milan)

Milan's luxury hotels and resorts offer an unparalleled level of comfort, elegance, and sophistication for discerning travelers seeking an unforgettable experience in the heart of the city. From historic landmarks to modern marvels, these six establishments redefine luxury accommodation in Milan, promising an indulgent retreat in the midst of one of Europe's most vibrant cities. Whether you're seeking Michelin-starred dining, personalized services, or world-class amenities, Milan's luxury hotels have something to offer for every discerning traveler.

2.2 Boutique and Design Hotels

Milan, renowned for its fashion, design, and innovation, is home to a plethora of boutique and design hotels that cater to travelers seeking a unique and stylish accommodation experience. These six establishments showcase the city's creative flair and offer a blend of luxury, comfort, and cutting-edge design.

Hotel VIU Milan

Located in the vibrant Porta Volta district, Hotel VIU Milan is a stylish haven for design aficionados and luxury travelers. Prices for lodging start at €300 per night for a deluxe room, with suites available from €600 per night. Each room and suite boasts contemporary design, sleek furnishings, and floor-to-ceiling windows offering panoramic views of the city skyline. Guests can unwind at the hotel's rooftop pool and bar, indulge in gourmet cuisine at the Michelin-starred restaurant, or relax with a spa treatment at the wellness center. Special services include personalized concierge assistance, complimentary bike rentals, and access to exclusive events and experiences. Prices for meals range from €30 to €100 per person. For reservations and bookings, visit the official website at (www.hotelviumilan.com).

Room Mate Giulia

Situated in the heart of Milan's historic center, Room Mate Giulia is a chic and contemporary boutique hotel that combines Italian elegance with modern design. Prices for lodging start at €200 per night for a standard room, with suites available from €400 per night. Each room and suite features stylish decor, vibrant colors, and state-of-the-art amenities. Guests can enjoy a complimentary buffet breakfast served in the hotel's stylish dining room, relax in the cozy lounge area, or borrow a bike to explore the city. Special services include personalized concierge assistance, airport transfers, and pet-friendly accommodations. Prices for meals range from €20 to €50 per person. For reservations and bookings, visit the official website at (www.room-matehotels.com/en/giulia).

STRAFhotel&bar

Located in the heart of Milan's fashion district, STRAFhotel&bar is a design-centric hotel that celebrates the city's creative spirit and artistic heritage. Prices for lodging start at €250 per night for a standard room, with suites available from €500 per night. Each room and suite is uniquely decorated with contemporary furnishings, bold colors, and avant-garde artwork. Guests can unwind at the hotel's stylish bar, enjoy a cocktail crafted by expert mixologists, or dine at the Michelin-recommended restaurant. Special services include personalized concierge assistance, complimentary Wi-Fi, and access to the hotel's fitness center. Prices for meals range from €30 to €80 per person. For reservations and bookings, visit the official website at (www.straf.it/en/)

Hotel Milano Scala

Situated in the heart of Milan's historic Brera district, Hotel Milano Scala is a boutique hotel that combines classic elegance with eco-friendly design. Prices for lodging start at €200 per night for a classic room, with suites available from €400 per night. Each room and suite features sustainable furnishings, organic bedding, and energy-efficient amenities. Guests can enjoy a complimentary buffet breakfast served in the hotel's scenic courtyard, relax in the cozy library lounge, or attend a live music performance at the hotel's concert hall. Special services include personalized wellness programs, guided tours of Milan's cultural landmarks, and access to the hotel's rooftop terrace. Prices for meals range from €20 to €50 per person. For reservations and bookings, visit the official website at (www.hotelmilanoscala.it/en/).

TownHouse Galleria

Housed within the iconic Galleria Vittorio Emanuele II, TownHouse Galleria is a luxurious boutique hotel that offers unparalleled views of Milan's historic landmarks. Prices for lodging start at €500 per night for a deluxe room, with suites available from €1,000 per night. Each room and suite boasts elegant decor, modern amenities, and stunning views of the Galleria's soaring glass dome. Guests can dine at the hotel's gourmet restaurant, enjoy a cocktail at the stylish bar, or indulge in a spa treatment at the wellness center. Special services include personalized shopping experiences, private guided tours, and access to exclusive events and exhibitions. Prices for meals range from €50 to €200 per person. For reservations and bookings, visit the official website at (www.townhousegalleria.com/en/)

The Yard Milano

Nestled in the vibrant Navigli district, The Yard Milano is a boutique hotel that offers a blend of contemporary design and historic charm. Prices for lodging start at €150 per night for a standard room, with suites available from €300 per night. Each room and suite features stylish decor, modern amenities, and unique architectural details. Guests can relax in the hotel's tranquil courtyard garden, enjoy a cocktail at the bar, or borrow a book from the library. Special services include personalized concierge assistance, bike rentals, and access to the hotel's fitness center. Prices for meals range from €20 to €50 per person. For reservations and bookings, visit the official website at (www.theyardmilano.com/en/). Milan's boutique and design hotels offer a stylish and immersive accommodation experience for travelers seeking a blend of luxury, comfort, and creativity. From chic boutique hotels in the heart of the city to design-centric establishments in historic landmarks, these establishments showcase Milan's vibrant cultural scene and celebrate its rich heritage. Whether you're exploring the city's historic landmarks, indulging in its culinary delights, or immersing yourself in its vibrant arts scene, Milan offers something for every traveler to enjoy, Milan offers something for every traveler to enjoy. Milan's boutique and design hotels provide the perfect backdrop for an unforgettable stay in one of Europe's most stylish cities.

2.3 Budget-Friendly Accommodations

Milan, a city known for its high fashion and luxury lifestyle, also offers a range of budget-friendly accommodation options for travelers looking to explore the city without breaking the bank. These six establishments provide comfortable lodging, convenient locations, and wallet-friendly prices, ensuring a memorable stay in the vibrant heart of Milan.

Ostello Bello Grande

Nestled in the lively Navigli district, Ostello Bello Grande offers affordable accommodations with a vibrant and social atmosphere. Prices for lodging start at €30 per night for a dormitory bed, with private rooms available from €80 per night. Each room is cozy and comfortable, with modern amenities and complimentary Wi-Fi. Guests can enjoy a complimentary buffet breakfast served in the hostel's communal kitchen, relax in the cozy lounge area, or socialize with fellow travelers in the rooftop garden. Special services include guided walking tours, bike rentals, and nightly events such as live music and movie screenings. Prices for meals vary, with affordable options available in the hostel's restaurant and bar. For reservations and bookings, visit the official website at (www.ostellobello.com/en/grande/).

Meininger Milano Lambrate

Conveniently located near Lambrate train station, Meininger Milano Lambrate offers budget-friendly accommodations with modern amenities and a relaxed atmosphere. Prices for lodging start at €40 per night for a dormitory bed, with private rooms available from €80 per night. Each room is spacious and well-equipped, with comfortable beds, en-suite bathrooms, and free Wi-Fi. Guests can enjoy a continental breakfast buffet served in the hotel's dining area, relax in the cozy lounge, or play games in the game room. Special services include bike rentals, luggage storage, and a 24-hour reception desk. Prices for meals vary, with affordable options available in the hotel's cafe and bar. For reservations and bookings, visit the official website at (www.meininger-hotels.com/en/hotels/milan/milan-lambrate/).

New Generation Hostel Urban Città Studi

Located in the bustling Città Studi neighborhood, New Generation Hostel Urban Città Studi offers affordable accommodations with a youthful and energetic vibe. Prices for lodging start at €20 per night for a dormitory bed, with private rooms available from €60 per night. Each room is simple and functional, with comfortable beds, individual lockers, and free Wi-Fi. Guests can enjoy a continental breakfast served in the hostel's dining area, relax in the cozy lounge, or socialize with fellow travelers in the outdoor courtyard. Special services include bike rentals, laundry facilities, and a 24-hour front desk. Prices for meals vary, with affordable options available in the hostel's cafe and vending machines. For reservations and bookings, visit the official website at (www.newgenerationhostel.com/en/milan/citta-studi/)

Hotel Berna

Situated near Milan Central Station, Hotel Berna offers budget-friendly accommodations with a focus on comfort and convenience. Prices for lodging start at €60 per night for a standard room, with deluxe rooms available from €100 per night.Each room is tastefully adorned and equipped with modern amenities, including complimentary Wi-Fi access.i. Guests can enjoy a complimentary buffet breakfast served in the hotel's breakfast room, relax in the cozy lounge area, or borrow a book from the hotel's library. Special services include airport transfers, luggage storage, and a 24-hour front desk. Prices for meals vary, with affordable options available in the hotel's restaurant and bar. For reservations and bookings, visit the official website at (www.hotelberna.com/en/).

Hotel Arizona

Located near Loreto metro station, Hotel Arizona offers affordable accommodations with a focus on simplicity and comfort. Prices for lodging start at €50 per night for a standard room, with superior rooms available from €80 per night. Each room is cozy and functional, with modern amenities and free Wi-Fi. Guests can enjoy a continental breakfast served in the hotel's breakfast room, relax in the cozy lounge area, or unwind on the outdoor terrace. Special services include luggage storage, ticket assistance, and a 24-hour front desk. Prices for meals vary, with affordable options available in the hotel's cafe and nearby restaurants. For reservations and bookings, visit the official website at (www.hotel-arizona-milan.com/en/).

Hotel Charly

Situated in the vibrant Porta Venezia neighborhood, Hotel Charly offers affordable accommodations with a friendly and welcoming atmosphere. Prices for lodging start at

€40 per night for a standard room, with superior rooms available from €70 per night. Each room is comfortable and well-equipped, with modern amenities and free Wi-Fi. Guests can enjoy a continental breakfast served in the hotel's breakfast room, relax in the cozy lounge area, or rent a bike to explore the city. Special services include luggage storage, airport transfers, and a 24-hour front desk. Prices for meals vary, with affordable options available in the hotel's cafe and nearby eateries. For reservations and bookings, visit the official website at (www.hotelcharlymilan.com/en/)

Milan's budget-friendly accommodation options offer travelers the opportunity to experience the city's vibrant culture, history, and lifestyle without breaking the bank. From hostels with social atmospheres to budget hotels with modern amenities, these six establishments provide comfortable lodging, convenient locations, and wallet-friendly prices, ensuring a memorable stay in the heart of Milan. Whether you're exploring the city's historic landmarks, indulging in its culinary delights, or immersing yourself in its vibrant arts scene, Milan offers something for every traveler to enjoy. Milan's budget-friendly accommodations provide the perfect base for an unforgettable adventure in one of Europe's most dynamic cities.

2.4 Bed and Breakfasts

When it comes to experiencing the warmth and hospitality of Milan, bed and breakfast accommodations offer a charming alternative to traditional hotels. These six establishments provide cozy and intimate settings, personalized service, and a taste of authentic Milanese living for travelers seeking a more intimate and homey experience.

Hemeras Boutique House

Located in the heart of Milan's historic center, Hemeras Boutique House offers a collection of beautifully appointed apartments designed for comfort and style. Prices for lodging start at €100 per night for a studio apartment, with larger apartments available from €150 per night. Each apartment features elegant decor, modern amenities, and fully equipped kitchens, providing guests with the freedom to create their own home-away-from-home experience. Guests can enjoy a continental breakfast delivered to their apartment each morning, relax in the cozy living area, or take advantage of the concierge service to arrange personalized experiences and activities. Prices for meals vary, with guests able to explore nearby cafes and restaurants or cook their own meals in the apartment's kitchen. For reservations and bookings, visit the official website at (www.hemerasboutiquehouse.com/en/).

Petit Palais Hotel de Charme
Situated in the picturesque Brera district, Petit Palais Hotel de Charme is a quaint bed and breakfast housed in a historic building dating back to the 19th century. Prices for lodging start at €120 per night for a standard room, with deluxe rooms available from €180 per night. Each room is elegantly decorated with antique furnishings, luxurious linens, and modern amenities, offering guests a cozy and intimate retreat in the heart of Milan. Guests can enjoy a continental breakfast served in the hotel's charming dining room, relax in the cozy lounge area, or take a leisurely stroll through the hotel's tranquil courtyard garden. Special services include personalized concierge assistance, bike rentals, and guided tours of the city's landmarks and attractions. Prices for meals vary, with guests able to explore nearby cafes and restaurants or enjoy a meal in the hotel's dining room. For reservations and bookings, visit the official website at (www.petitpalais.it/en/)

Hotel Gran Duca di York
Located in a historic building near Milan's Duomo Cathedral, Hotel Gran Duca di York is a charming bed and breakfast that exudes old-world elegance and charm. Prices for lodging start at €90 per night for a standard room, with deluxe rooms available from €150 per night. Each room is tastefully decorated with antique furnishings, plush bedding, and modern amenities, providing guests with a cozy and comfortable retreat in the heart of the city. Guests can enjoy a continental breakfast served in the hotel's elegant dining room, relax in the cozy lounge area, or take advantage of the hotel's concierge service to arrange personalized experiences and activities. Prices for meals vary, with guests able to explore nearby cafes and restaurants or enjoy a meal in the

hotel's dining room. For reservations and bookings, visit the official website at (www.granducadiyork.com/en/).

Locanda ai Due Orsi

Nestled in the charming Navigli district, Locanda ai Due Orsi is a cozy bed and breakfast housed in a historic building dating back to the 18th century. Prices for lodging start at €80 per night for a standard room, with deluxe rooms available from €120 per night. Each room is individually decorated with rustic furnishings, warm colors, and modern amenities, offering guests a cozy and intimate retreat in the heart of Milan. Guests can enjoy a continental breakfast served in the hotel's charming dining room, relax in the cozy lounge area, or take a leisurely stroll along the nearby canals. Special services include personalized concierge assistance, bike rentals, and guided tours of the city's landmarks and attractions. Prices for meals vary, with guests able to explore nearby cafes and restaurants or enjoy a meal in the hotel's dining room. For reservations and bookings, visit the official website at www.locandaidueorsi.it/en/)

Brera Apartments

Situated in the trendy Brera district, Brera Apartments offers a collection of stylish and contemporary apartments designed for comfort and convenience. Prices for lodging start at €80 per night for a studio apartment, with larger apartments available from €150 per night. Each apartment features modern decor, fully equipped kitchens, and spacious living areas, providing guests with a home-away-from-home experience in the heart of Milan. Guests can enjoy a continental breakfast delivered to their apartment each morning, relax on the private terrace or balcony, or take advantage of the concierge service to arrange personalized experiences and activities. Prices for meals vary, with guests able to explore nearby cafes and restaurants or cook their own meals in the apartment's kitchen. For reservations and bookings, visit the official website at (www.brera-apartments.com/en/).

B&B La Villetta

Located in the peaceful Porta Romana district, B&B La Villetta is a charming bed and breakfast surrounded by lush gardens and greenery. Prices for lodging start at €70 per night for a standard room, with deluxe rooms available from €120 per night. Each room is cozy and comfortable, with simple decor, comfortable furnishings, and modern amenities, providing guests with a peaceful escape from the city's hustle and bustle. Guests can enjoy a continental breakfast served in the hotel's charming dining room or outdoor terrace, relax in the peaceful garden area, or explore the nearby parks and green spaces. Special services include personalized concierge assistance, bike rentals, and guided tours of the city's landmarks and attractions. Prices for meals vary, with guests able to explore nearby cafes and restaurants or enjoy a meal in the hotel's dining room. For reservations and bookings, visit the official website at (www.bblavilletta.com/en/). Milan's bed and breakfast accommodations offer travelers a charming and intimate alternative to traditional hotels, providing cozy and comfortable retreats in the heart of the city. From historic buildings to contemporary apartments, these six establishments showcase Milan's warm hospitality, authentic charm, and unique character, ensuring a memorable and enjoyable stay for guests seeking a more personal and homey experience in one of Europe's most vibrant cities.

2.5 Unique Stays: Apartments and Guesthouses

In a city as vibrant and diverse as Milan, exploring its hidden gems often requires staying in unique accommodations that offer a glimpse into the city's authentic charm and character. These six establishments provide guests with the opportunity to experience Milan like a local, offering distinctive stays in apartments and guest houses that are as memorable as they are comfortable.

Temporary House - Milan Fashion District

Located in the heart of Milan's fashion district, Temporary House offers a collection of stylish and contemporary apartments designed for modern travelers. Prices for lodging start at €100 per night for a studio apartment, with larger apartments available from €150 per night. Each apartment features sleek and modern decor, fully equipped kitchens, and spacious living areas, providing guests with a comfortable and convenient home-away-from-home experience. Guests can enjoy complimentary Wi-Fi, access to a fitness center, and personalized concierge services to help plan their stay in Milan. Special services include airport transfers, grocery delivery, and guided tours of the city's fashion landmarks. Prices for meals vary, with guests able to explore nearby cafes and restaurants or cook their own meals in the apartment's kitchen. For reservations and bookings, visit the official website at (www.temporaryhousemilan.com/en/).

Suite Milano Duomo

Situated just steps away from Milan's iconic Duomo Cathedral, Suite Milano Duomo offers guests the opportunity to stay in a historic building with modern comforts and amenities. Prices for lodging start at €150 per night for a standard suite, with deluxe suites available from €250 per night. Each suite is elegantly decorated with luxurious furnishings, plush bedding, and modern amenities, offering guests a cozy and intimate retreat in the heart of the city. Guests can enjoy complimentary breakfast served in the suite, relax in the spacious living area, or take in panoramic views of the city from the rooftop terrace. Special services include personalized concierge assistance, private guided tours, and access to exclusive events and exhibitions. Prices for meals vary, with guests able to explore nearby cafes and restaurants or enjoy a meal in the suite's dining area. For reservations and bookings, visit the official website at (www.suitemilanoduomo.com/en/).

The Street Milano Duomo

Located in a historic building near Milan's Duomo Cathedral, The Street Milano Duomo offers guests a unique and memorable stay in the heart of the city. Prices for lodging start at €120 per night for a standard room, with deluxe rooms available from €200 per night. Each room is tastefully decorated with contemporary furnishings, vibrant colors, and modern amenities, providing guests with a comfortable and stylish retreat in the midst of Milan's bustling streets. Guests can enjoy complimentary breakfast served in the hotel's charming dining room, relax in the cozy lounge area, or take advantage of the hotel's concierge service to arrange personalized experiences and activities. Special services include airport transfers, luggage storage, and a 24-hour front desk. Prices for meals vary, with guests able to explore nearby cafes and restaurants or enjoy a meal in the hotel's dining room. For reservations and bookings, visit the official website at (www.thestreetmilanoduomo.com/en/).

Style Apartments Milano

Situated in the trendy Brera district, Style Apartments Milano offers guests the opportunity to stay in chic and contemporary apartments with modern amenities and personalized service. Prices for lodging start at €100 per night for a studio apartment, with larger apartments available from €200 per night. Each apartment features stylish decor, fully equipped kitchens, and spacious living areas, providing guests with a comfortable and convenient home-away-from-home experience. Guests can enjoy complimentary Wi-Fi, access to a fitness center, and personalized concierge services to help plan their stay in Milan. Special services include airport transfers, grocery delivery, and guided tours of the city's cultural landmarks. Prices for meals vary, with guests able to explore nearby cafes and restaurants or cook their own meals in the apartment's kitchen. For reservations and bookings, visit the official website at (www.styleapartmentsmilano.com/en/).

Heart Milan Apartments

Nestled in the charming Navigli district, Heart Milan Apartments offers guests the opportunity to stay in stylish and modern apartments with stunning views of the city's historic canals. Prices for lodging start at €80 per night for a studio apartment, with larger apartments available from €150 per night. Each apartment features contemporary decor, fully equipped kitchens, and spacious living areas, providing guests with a comfortable and convenient retreat in the heart of Milan. Guests can enjoy complimentary Wi-Fi, access to a fitness center, and personalized concierge services to help plan their stay in Milan. Special services include airport transfers, grocery delivery, and guided tours of the city's cultural landmarks. Prices for meals vary, with guests able to explore nearby cafes and restaurants or cook their own meals in the apartment's kitchen. For reservations and bookings, visit the official website at (www.heartmilanapartments.com/en/).

B&B Milano Bella

Located in a historic building near Milan's Porta Venezia district, B&B Milano Bella offers guests a cozy and intimate stay in a charming guest house setting. Prices for lodging start at €80 per night for a standard room, with deluxe rooms available from €150 per night.Each room is tastefully adorned with stylish furnishings, luxurious bedding, and contemporary amenities. providing guests with a comfortable and relaxing retreat in the heart of Milan. Guests can enjoy a continental breakfast served in the guest house's charming dining room, relax in the cozy lounge area, or take advantage of the concierge service to arrange personalized experiences and activities. Special services include airport transfers, luggage storage, and a 24-hour front desk. Prices for meals vary, with guests able to explore nearby cafes and restaurants or enjoy a meal in the guest house's dining room. For reservations and bookings, visit the official website at (www.bbmilanobella.com/en/).

Milan's unique stays in apartments and guest houses offer travelers the opportunity to experience the city like a local, providing comfortable and stylish accommodations in the heart of the city's most vibrant neighborhoods. From historic buildings to contemporary apartments, these six establishments showcase Milan's authentic charm, cultural diversity, and rich heritage, ensuring a memorable and enjoyable stay for guests seeking a distinctive and immersive experience in one of Europe's most dynamic cities.

CHAPTER 3
TRANSPORTATION IN MILAN

3.1 Public Transport Networks

Milan, the bustling metropolis in northern Italy, boasts an extensive and efficient public transportation network that caters to the needs of its residents and visitors alike. From trams to buses, metro lines to suburban trains, Milan offers a variety of options for getting around the city conveniently and affordably.

Metro System

The backbone of Milan's public transportation network is its metro system, comprising four lines: M1 (red line), M2 (green line), M3 (yellow line), and M5 (lilac line). Each line covers different areas of the city, intersecting at key transfer stations such as Duomo, Cadorna, and Centrale. The metro operates from around 6:00 AM until midnight, with slightly extended hours on weekends and holidays.

Trams

Milan is renowned for its iconic tram network, which provides an atmospheric and scenic mode of transport through the city streets. Trams crisscross Milan, reaching areas not accessible by the metro. With over 20 lines, visitors can explore various neighborhoods and attractions conveniently. Trams generally operate from early morning until midnight, with frequency depending on the specific line and time of day.

Buses

Complementing the metro and tram systems, Milan's bus network offers extensive coverage, connecting neighborhoods, suburbs, and peripheral areas. Visitors can rely on buses to reach destinations not served by other modes of public transportation. Milan's buses operate throughout the day and into the evening, with varying frequencies depending on the route.

Suburban Trains (Passante Ferroviario)

The Passante Ferroviario, Milan's suburban rail network, provides rapid transit services connecting the city center with outlying districts and neighboring towns. Visitors can use suburban trains to reach destinations beyond the city limits, including popular tourist spots such as Lake Como and Monza. The Passante Ferroviario operates from early morning until late evening, with frequent services on weekdays and reduced schedules on weekends.

Ticketing and Prices

Milan's public transportation system operates on an integrated fare system managed by ATM (Azienda Trasporti Milanesi), the city's public transport authority. Visitors can purchase tickets and travel passes from various points of sale, including ticket vending machines at metro stations, authorized resellers, and online platforms. Single tickets are valid for 90 minutes from the time of validation and allow unlimited transfers within that timeframe across all modes of public transportation. There are also options for multiple-ride tickets, daily passes, and weekly or monthly subscriptions, providing flexibility for visitors staying longer in Milan.

Navigating Effectively

To navigate Milan's public transportation network effectively, visitors can utilize several resources:

Transport Maps: Maps of the metro, tram, and bus networks are readily available at metro stations, tourist information centers, and online. These maps highlight key routes, transfer stations, and major attractions, aiding visitors in planning their journeys.

Journey Planner Apps: Smartphone apps such as Google Maps, Moovit, and the official ATM Milano app offer real-time information on routes, schedules, and estimated travel times. Visitors can input their starting point and destination to receive detailed transit directions, making it easy to navigate the city.

Timetables and Signage: Paying attention to timetables posted at bus and tram stops, as well as inside metro stations, helps visitors anticipate arrival times and plan their trips accordingly. Clear signage throughout the public transportation network also assists in navigating stations and platforms.

Ticket Validation: It's essential for visitors to validate their tickets upon boarding trams or buses and entering the metro system to avoid fines. Validation machines are typically located onboard trams and buses or at the entrances to metro stations. Milan's public transportation network offers visitors a comprehensive and efficient means of exploring the city and its surrounding areas. With a variety of options including metro, tram, bus, and suburban trains, coupled with user-friendly ticketing systems and navigation aids, travelers can navigate Milan with ease and convenience, making the most of their time in this vibrant Italian city.

3.2 Taxis and Ride-Sharing Services

Transportation is essential in the daily routines of individuals worldwide. Taxis and ride-sharing services have become popular choices for travel due to their convenience and accessibility. These options provide unique benefits, meeting a variety of preferences and requirements. In this comprehensive guide, we will delve into the nuances of taxis and ride-sharing services, exploring their features, benefits, and key players in the industry.

Taxis

Taxis, synonymous with convenience and flexibility, have been a staple in urban transportation for decades. These vehicles, typically operated by licensed drivers, provide on-demand services, allowing passengers to hail a ride spontaneously or book in advance. Taxis offer a direct point-to-point service, eliminating the need for multiple stops commonly associated with public transit. In addition to street pickups, many taxi companies now offer mobile apps for seamless booking and payment.

Key Taxi Companies

Yellow Cab Co.: Established in numerous cities worldwide, including New York, London, and Tokyo, Yellow Cab Co. boasts a fleet of well-maintained vehicles and experienced drivers. Contact: Website: yellowcab.com | Phone: +1-800-609-8731

Uber Taxi: Uber, a pioneer in the ride-hailing industry, also offers traditional taxi services in select cities. With its user-friendly app, passengers can easily request a taxi and track its arrival in real-time. Contact: Website: uber.com | Phone: Varies by location

City Taxis: Serving cities across Europe, City Taxis provides reliable transportation with a focus on customer satisfaction. Whether for short trips or airport transfers, their drivers prioritize safety and efficiency. Contact: Website: citytaxis.com | Phone: Varies by location

Ride-Sharing Services

Ride-sharing services revolutionized urban transportation, offering a cost-effective alternative to traditional taxis. These platforms facilitate connections between passengers and independent drivers via mobile applications, enabling peer-to-peer transactions. Ride-sharing promotes resource sharing, reducing congestion and environmental impact while providing flexible income opportunities for drivers.

Key Ride-Sharing Companies

Uber: Uber remains a dominant force in the ride-sharing market, operating in numerous cities worldwide. Passengers can choose from various ride options, including economy, premium, and shared rides, tailored to their preferences and budget. Contact: Website: uber.com | Phone: Varies by location

Lyft: Lyft, known for its emphasis on community and social responsibility, offers ride-sharing services in major cities across the United States and Canada. Passengers appreciate Lyft's transparent pricing and commitment to safety. Contact: Website: lyft.com | Phone: Varies by location

Didi Chuxing: Didi Chuxing, based in China, is one of the largest ride-sharing companies globally, providing services in over 400 cities. With its advanced technology and extensive network, Didi offers a seamless travel experience for millions of passengers daily. Contact: Website: didiglobal.com | Phone: Varies by location

Comparative Analysis

When comparing taxis and ride-sharing services, several factors come into play. Taxis offer the advantage of immediate availability and curbside pickups, ideal for spontaneous travel or in areas with limited public transit access. However, ride-sharing services often provide lower fares and greater convenience through app-based booking and cashless transactions. Taxis and ride-sharing services complement each other, catering to diverse transportation needs in urban environments. Whether opting for the familiarity of a traditional taxi or the affordability of a ride-sharing service, passengers can expect convenience, reliability, and flexibility. By understanding the features and key players in both sectors, visitors can make informed decisions to enhance their travel experiences.

3.3 Renting a Car or Bike

Milan welcomes visitors from around the globe. While the city boasts an efficient public transportation system, many travelers prefer the freedom and flexibility of exploring on their terms. Car and bike rentals offer convenient options for navigating Milan and its surrounding areas, allowing visitors to delve deeper into its hidden gems and iconic landmarks.

Car Rentals in Milan

Car rentals in Milan cater to diverse needs, whether for leisurely drives through the picturesque countryside or convenient urban exploration. Several reputable rental companies operate throughout the city, offering a range of vehicles to suit varying preferences and budgets.

Key Car Rental Companies

Hertz Car Rental: With multiple locations across Milan, including airports and downtown areas, Hertz Car Rental provides a wide selection of vehicles, from compact cars to luxury sedans. For bookings visit: *hertz.com*

Avis Rent a Car: Avis Rent a Car offers convenient pickup and drop-off locations throughout Milan, ensuring hassle-free rental experiences for visitors. Whether for short-term or long-term rentals, Avis provides competitive rates and excellent customer service. For bookings: *avis.com*

Europcar Milan: Europcar Milan boasts a comprehensive fleet of vehicles, including environmentally-friendly options, suitable for eco-conscious travelers. With flexible rental agreements and convenient online booking, Europcar simplifies the process of exploring Milan and beyond. For bookings visit: *europcar.com*

Bike Rentals in Milan

For those seeking a more eco-friendly and leisurely mode of transportation, bike rentals offer an excellent alternative in Milan. The city's flat terrain and extensive network of bike lanes make it ideal for cycling enthusiasts of all levels.

Key Bike Rental Companies

BikeMi: Operated by the City of Milan, BikeMi provides a convenient bike-sharing system with numerous stations located throughout the city. Visitors can easily register online or at kiosks to access bikes for short-term rentals, making it an ideal option for spontaneous exploration. For bookings visit:: *bikemi.com*

Milano Bike Rental: Milano Bike Rental offers a range of bicycles, including traditional bikes, electric bikes, and tandem bikes, catering to individual preferences and group outings. With flexible rental durations and competitive rates, Milano Bike Rental provides an enjoyable and eco-friendly way to discover Milan's sights. For bookings visit; *milanobikerental.com*

Bike Rent Milan: Bike Rent Milan specializes in providing high-quality bikes for rent, along with optional accessories such as helmets, locks, and baskets. Located near popular tourist attractions, their rental shops offer convenient pickup and drop-off services, ensuring a seamless cycling experience for visitors. For bookings visit: *bikerentmilan.com*

Prices and Additional Information

Prices for car rentals in Milan vary depending on factors such as vehicle type, rental duration, and insurance coverage. Generally, rates start at around €30-40 per day for compact cars and can increase for larger or luxury vehicles. Similarly, bike rental prices in Milan range from €5-15 per hour or €15-30 per day, with discounts available for longer rental periods or group bookings. Most rental companies require a valid ID, security deposit, and signed rental agreement upon pickup. In addition to rental fees, visitors should consider additional costs such as fuel, tolls, parking fees, and optional insurance coverage. It's advisable to inquire about specific terms and conditions, including mileage limits, insurance coverage, and rental policies, before confirming reservations. Whether opting for the convenience of a rental car or the eco-friendly appeal of a bike, visitors to Milan have ample options for exploring the city and its surrounding areas. By choosing reputable rental companies and understanding pricing structures and rental policies, travelers can enjoy seamless and memorable experiences as they navigate Milan's vibrant streets and iconic landmarks.

3.4 Walking Tours and Guided Transportation

Milan offers visitors an array of options to explore its vibrant streets and iconic landmarks. Walking tours and guided transportation provide unique opportunities to delve deeper into Milan's rich tapestry, offering insightful narratives and personalized experiences tailored to diverse interests and preferences.

Walking Tours in Milan

Walking tours offer an intimate and immersive way to discover Milan's hidden gems and storied past. Led by knowledgeable guides, these tours provide fascinating insights into the city's history, art, and culture, while traversing its charming neighborhoods and bustling squares.

Variety of Walking Tours

Historical Walking Tours: Explore Milan's historic center, including the magnificent Duomo Cathedral, La Scala Opera House, and Sforza Castle. These tours delve into the city's rich heritage, highlighting significant landmarks and architectural masterpieces.

Art and Culture Walking Tours: Delve into Milan's artistic legacy with tours focused on renowned art galleries, such as the Pinacoteca di Brera, and contemporary art districts like the Isola neighborhood. Visitors can admire masterpieces by Italian masters and discover emerging talent in Milan's vibrant art scene.

Food and Wine Walking Tours: Embark on culinary adventures through Milan's gastronomic hotspots, sampling local delicacies, artisanal cheeses, and fine wines. These tours offer a tantalizing journey for food enthusiasts, showcasing Milan's diverse culinary landscape and culinary traditions.

Guided Transportation in Milan

Guided transportation provides convenient and efficient ways to navigate Milan's sprawling metropolis, ensuring seamless travel experiences for visitors. From hop-on-hop-off buses to guided boat tours along the Navigli canals, these transportation options offer panoramic views and informative commentary, enhancing the sightseeing experience.

Variety of Guided Transportation

Hop-on-Hop-off Bus Tours: Explore Milan's major attractions at your own pace with hop-on-hop-off bus tours, which provide flexible transportation between key landmarks, including the Duomo, the Last Supper, and the fashion district. Passengers can disembark at any stop to explore nearby sights before hopping back on the bus to continue their journey.

Guided Boat Tours: Discover Milan's picturesque waterways and historic canals with guided boat tours along the Navigli district. Visitors can admire charming waterfronts, historic bridges, and lively cafes while learning about Milan's maritime heritage and urban development.

Segway Tours: Experience Milan's sights from a unique perspective with guided Segway tours, offering thrilling rides through the city's streets and squares. Led by experienced instructors, these tours provide an exhilarating way to cover more ground while stopping at notable landmarks along the way.

Navigating Effectively with Walking Tours and Guided Transportation

To make the most of walking tours and guided transportation in Milan, visitors can follow these tips

Plan Ahead: Research available tours and transportation options in advance, considering interests, schedules, and budgetary constraints.

Book in Advance: Secure reservations for preferred walking tours and guided transportation services to guarantee availability, especially during peak tourist seasons.

Stay Informed: Pay attention to tour itineraries, meeting points, and departure times to ensure timely arrival and departure.

Engage with Guides: Take advantage of opportunities to interact with knowledgeable guides, asking questions and seeking recommendations for additional sights or activities.

Remain Flexible: Be open to unexpected discoveries and spontaneous detours while exploring Milan's vibrant streets and neighborhoods. Walking tours and guided transportation offer enriching experiences for visitors eager to explore Milan's diverse cultural offerings and architectural marvels. Whether strolling through historic squares, cruising along scenic waterways, or gliding through the city on a Segway, travelers can immerse themselves in Milan's vibrant atmosphere while gaining deeper insights into its captivating history and heritage. By embracing these opportunities for exploration and discovery, visitors can create lasting memories of their time in this dynamic city.

3.5 Accessibility Considerations for Travelers

Ensuring accessibility for all travelers is essential for creating inclusive and welcoming environments in cities like Milan. Whether exploring cultural landmarks, navigating public transportation, or enjoying local amenities, visitors with disabilities or mobility challenges require thoughtful accommodations to fully experience the city's offerings. Here are six key accessibility considerations for travelers in Milan:

Accessible Accommodation

When selecting accommodations in Milan, travelers should prioritize hotels, guesthouses, or rental properties that offer accessible features such as wheelchair-accessible rooms, elevators with braille signage, and accessible bathrooms. Many hotels in Milan have adapted rooms equipped with grab bars, roll-in showers, and widened doorways to accommodate guests with mobility impairments.

Barrier-Free Attractions

Milan boasts a wealth of cultural attractions, from historic landmarks to contemporary museums, and ensuring their accessibility is paramount. Visitors should research attractions in advance to identify those with barrier-free access, including wheelchair ramps, elevators, and accessible restrooms. Many museums and galleries in Milan offer priority entrance and guided tours for visitors with disabilities.

Accessible Transportation

Navigating Milan's transportation system can be made easier with accessible options for travelers with mobility challenges. The city's metro stations are equipped with elevators and tactile paving to assist visually impaired passengers. Additionally, buses and trams feature low-floor boarding and designated spaces for wheelchair users. Visitors can inquire about accessible transportation options, including taxi services equipped with wheelchair ramps or lifts.

Accessible Dining and Entertainment

When dining out or enjoying entertainment venues in Milan, travelers should seek establishments with accessible facilities and services. Restaurants with step-free entrances, spacious seating areas, and accessible restrooms ensure a comfortable dining experience for all guests. Similarly, theaters, cinemas, and concert halls offering accessible seating arrangements and assistive listening devices enhance inclusivity for patrons with disabilities.

Accessible Streets and Sidewalks

Exploring Milan's vibrant streets and neighborhoods is made easier with accessible pathways and pedestrian infrastructure. Visitors should be mindful of uneven surfaces, cobblestone streets, and narrow sidewalks that may pose challenges for travelers with mobility impairments. Fortunately, many areas in Milan, particularly around tourist hotspots and shopping districts, have undergone accessibility improvements, including widened sidewalks and tactile paving.

Accessibility Information and Resources

To navigate Milan effectively, travelers should access comprehensive accessibility information and resources available online or through visitor centers. Websites and mobile apps provide valuable insights into accessible attractions, transportation options, and services in Milan. Additionally, visitor centers and tourist information offices can offer personalized assistance and recommendations tailored to travelers' specific needs and preferences.

Navigating Effectively with Accessibility Considerations in Milan

To maximize accessibility and ensure a seamless travel experience in Milan, visitors can follow these tips:

Plan Ahead: Research accessibility features and accommodations in advance to make informed decisions when booking accommodations, selecting attractions, and planning activities.

Communicate Needs: Clearly communicate any accessibility requirements or special assistance needs to hotels, transportation providers, and tour operators when making reservations or inquiries.

Utilize Assistive Devices: Take advantage of assistive devices and technologies such as mobility aids, hearing aids, and visual aids to enhance independence and navigation while exploring Milan.

Seek Assistance: Don't hesitate to ask for assistance from hotel staff, transportation personnel, or local residents if encountering barriers or challenges while navigating Milan's streets and attractions.

Advocate for Accessibility: Provide feedback to businesses, attractions, and city authorities on accessibility issues encountered during your visit, contributing to ongoing efforts to improve accessibility and inclusivity in Milan.

CHAPTER 4
TOP ATTRACTIONS/HIDDEN GEMS

Click the link or Scan QR Code with a device to view a comprehensive map of Top Attractions in Milan – https://shorturl.at/gksX5

4.1 Iconic Landmarks: Duomo di Milano, Sforza Castle, etc.

Milan, the dynamic metropolis of Italy's Lombardy region, is celebrated for its illustrious history, lively culture, and architectural marvels. Among its myriad attractions, several iconic landmarks stand out as must-see destinations for visitors eager to immerse themselves in Milan's storied past and timeless beauty. From the awe-inspiring Duomo di Milano to the majestic Sforza Castle, each landmark offers a captivating glimpse into Milan's illustrious heritage and cultural significance.

Duomo di Milano: A Symbol of Grandeur and Faith

The Duomo di Milano, Milan's majestic cathedral, is a masterpiece of Gothic architecture and one of the largest churches in the world. Located in the heart of the city, the cathedral's intricate facade, adorned with spires, statues, and ornate carvings, is a testament to centuries of craftsmanship and devotion. The Duomo di Milano is centrally located in Piazza del Duomo, easily accessible by public transportation, including metro, tram, and bus services. Visitors can reach the cathedral by taking the M1 or M3 metro lines to the Duomo station. While entry to the cathedral itself is free, there is a fee to access certain areas, such as the terraces and the archaeological area. The cathedral is open daily from morning until evening, with varying hours for different sections.

Visiting the Duomo di Milano is a truly immersive experience, offering the opportunity to marvel at its stunning architecture, intricate stained glass windows, and impressive interior decor. Climbing to the rooftop terraces provides panoramic views of the city skyline and the surrounding Alps, making it a highlight for visitors. Construction of the Duomo began in the 14th century and continued for over 600 years, reflecting the evolving architectural styles and artistic influences of each era. The cathedral's significance extends beyond its architectural grandeur, serving as a symbol of Milan's religious heritage and cultural identity. In addition to admiring the cathedral's exterior and interior, visitors can explore the archaeological area beneath the cathedral, which showcases ancient ruins dating back to Roman times. Ascending to the terraces via stairs or elevator offers breathtaking views of Milan's skyline and the opportunity to admire the intricate details of the cathedral up close.

Sforza Castle: A Renaissance Fortress Amidst Urban Splendor
Sforza Castle, a formidable fortress-turned-museum, stands as a testament to Milan's Renaissance heritage and aristocratic power. Located in Parco Sempione, the castle's imposing walls and fortified towers house a treasure trove of art, history, and cultural artifacts. Situated in Parco Sempione, Sforza Castle is easily accessible by public transportation, with nearby tram and bus stops. Visitors can also enjoy a leisurely stroll through the park, soaking in the scenic beauty of its lush gardens and tranquil lakes. Entry to Sforza Castle is typically free, though there may be a fee to access certain exhibitions or special collections within the museum. The castle is open daily, with varying hours for different sections and exhibits. Exploring Sforza Castle offers a captivating journey through Milan's Renaissance history, from its origins as a medieval fortress to its transformation into a cultural hub and artistic showcase. The castle's extensive collection of artwork, including masterpieces by Leonardo da Vinci and Michelangelo, provides insight into Milan's rich artistic legacy.

Built in the 15th century by the powerful Sforza family, the castle served as a seat of political power and a symbol of Milanese sovereignty. Over the centuries, it has undergone numerous renovations and expansions, reflecting the evolving tastes and ambitions of its successive rulers. Visitors to Sforza Castle can explore its various museums and galleries, which house an impressive array of art, artifacts, and historical relics. Highlights include the Museo d'Arte Antica, showcasing Renaissance masterpieces, and the Sala delle Asse, adorned with Leonardo da Vinci's iconic frescoes.

Other Iconic Landmarks in Milan

In addition to the Duomo di Milano and Sforza Castle, Milan boasts several other iconic landmarks that are worth visiting:

Galleria Vittorio Emanuele II: A magnificent shopping arcade known for its elegant architecture, glass dome, and luxury boutiques, located adjacent to the Duomo.

Teatro alla Scala: One of the world's most famous opera houses, renowned for its opulent interiors, world-class performances, and illustrious history.

Santa Maria delle Grazie: Home to Leonardo da Vinci's masterpiece, "The Last Supper," this church is a UNESCO World Heritage Site and a must-visit for art enthusiasts.

Brera Art Gallery: Housed in a former monastery, this museum features an impressive collection of Italian Renaissance art, including works by Caravaggio, Raphael, and Titian.

Milan's iconic landmarks offer a captivating journey through the city's rich history, cultural heritage, and architectural splendors. From the awe-inspiring Duomo di Milano to the majestic Sforza Castle and beyond, each landmark tells a story of Milan's past and present, inviting visitors to explore its timeless beauty and cultural treasures. Whether marveling at Gothic cathedrals, admiring Renaissance masterpieces, or strolling through historic castles, a visit to Milan's iconic landmarks promises an unforgettable experience filled with history, culture, and inspiration.

4.2 Hidden Gems: Off-the-Beaten-Path Discoveries

Milan, often celebrated for its iconic landmarks and bustling city life, also harbors a wealth of hidden gems waiting to be discovered by intrepid travelers. These off-the-beaten-path attractions offer a glimpse into the city's lesser-known wonders, providing a unique and enriching experience for visitors seeking to delve beyond the tourist trail. Here, we unveil six must-see hidden gems in Milan, each offering a captivating blend of history, culture, and charm.

Biblioteca Ambrosiana: A Literary Haven in the Heart of Milan

Nestled in the historic center of Milan, the Biblioteca Ambrosiana stands as a beacon of knowledge and culture amidst the city's vibrant streets. Located adjacent to the renowned Piazza Duomo, this hidden gem is easily accessible by public transportation or on foot. Entry to the Biblioteca Ambrosiana typically requires a nominal fee, granting visitors access to its vast collection of rare manuscripts, ancient texts, and priceless artworks. Founded in the late 16th century by Cardinal Federico Borromeo, the library holds historical significance as one of the oldest in Europe, housing treasures such as Leonardo da Vinci's famous Codex Atlanticus. Visitors to the Biblioteca Ambrosiana can embark on a journey through the annals of history, exploring its meticulously preserved halls and exhibition spaces. Additionally, the library hosts guided tours, lectures, and cultural events, providing visitors with insights into Milan's rich literary heritage.

Villa Necchi Campiglio: An Architectural Gem Amidst Urban Splendor

Tucked away amidst Milan's elegant residential neighborhoods, Villa Necchi Campiglio offers a glimpse into the city's golden era of architecture and design. Located near the bustling Corso Venezia, this hidden gem is easily accessible by public transportation or taxi. Entry to Villa Necchi Campiglio typically requires a guided tour, with tickets available for purchase at the villa's entrance. Designed by renowned architect Piero Portaluppi in the 1930s, the villa boasts a striking blend of Art Deco and Rationalist styles, showcasing exquisite interiors and lush gardens. Visitors to Villa Necchi Campiglio can admire its opulent furnishings, intricate detailing, and timeless elegance as they explore its well-preserved rooms and landscaped grounds. Additionally, the villa hosts temporary exhibitions, cultural events, and culinary experiences, offering visitors a multifaceted glimpse into Milan's cultural heritage.

San Bernardino alle Ossa: A Hidden Gem of Religious Architecture

Tucked away in the heart of Milan's historic district, San Bernardino alle Ossa stands as a testament to the city's rich religious heritage. Located near the bustling Piazza del Duomo, this hidden gem is easily accessible by public transportation or on foot. Entry to San Bernardino alle Ossa is typically free of charge, welcoming visitors to explore its awe-inspiring interior and atmospheric crypt. Originally built in the 14th century, the church is renowned for its macabre ossuary, adorned with intricate bone decorations and haunting frescoes. Visitors to San Bernardino alle Ossa can marvel at the church's ornate architecture, including its elaborate Baroque façade and celestial dome. Additionally, the crypt houses a small museum showcasing religious artifacts and historical relics, providing insights into Milan's spiritual legacy.

Fondazione Prada: A Contemporary Art Haven in Industrial Surroundings

Located amidst Milan's former industrial district, the Fondazione Prada offers a cutting-edge blend of contemporary art, architecture, and culture. Easily accessible by public transportation or taxi, this hidden gem is situated near the vibrant Porta Romana neighborhood. Entry to the Fondazione Prada typically requires a ticket purchase, granting visitors access to its eclectic collection of contemporary artworks, avant-garde exhibitions, and architectural marvels. Founded by the renowned fashion house Prada, the foundation occupies a sprawling complex of historic and modern buildings, including a striking gold-leafed tower designed by architect Rem Koolhaas. Visitors to the Fondazione Prada can explore its diverse exhibition spaces, outdoor installations, and landscaped gardens, immersing themselves in a dynamic fusion of art and culture. Additionally, the foundation hosts film screenings, lectures, and cultural events, fostering dialogue and creativity within Milan's artistic community.

Chiesa di San Maurizio al Monastero Maggiore: A Hidden Gem of Renaissance Art

Situated amidst Milan's bustling city center, the Chiesa di San Maurizio al Monastero Maggiore offers a serene oasis of Renaissance art and architecture. Located near the vibrant Corso Magenta, this hidden gem is easily accessible by public transportation or on foot. Entry to the Chiesa di San Maurizio al Monastero Maggiore is typically free of charge, allowing visitors to marvel at its exquisite frescoes, ornate chapels, and tranquil cloisters. Built in the 16th century on the site of a former Benedictine monastery, the church is renowned for its richly decorated interior, featuring masterpieces by artists such as Bernardino Luini and Giovanni Battista Crespi. Visitors to the Chiesa di San Maurizio al Monastero Maggiore can wander through its hallowed halls, admiring its intricate detailing and sacred artworks. Additionally, the church hosts regular religious services, concerts, and guided tours, providing visitors with a spiritual and cultural experience.

Bosco Verticale: A Vertical Forest Amidst Urban Skylines

Rising amidst Milan's modern skyline, the Bosco Verticale (Vertical Forest) offers a visionary approach to urban living and sustainability. Located in the vibrant Porta Nuova district, this architectural marvel is easily accessible by public transportation or taxi. Entry to the Bosco Verticale typically requires admittance to the surrounding residential complex, with guided tours available for visitors interested in exploring its innovative design and ecological features. Designed by architect Stefano Boeri, the twin towers of the Bosco Verticale are adorned with lush vegetation, creating a vertical forest that absorbs carbon dioxide, reduces air pollution, and provides habitat for wildlife. Visitors to the Bosco Verticale can marvel at its verdant façades, panoramic views of the city, and sustainable design principles. Additionally, the surrounding Porta Nuova district offers a wealth of dining, shopping, and cultural attractions, making it an ideal destination for a day of exploration in Milan's modern metropolis. Milan's hidden gems offer a captivating glimpse into the city's diverse history, culture, and innovation. Whether it's exploring the Biblioteca Ambrosiana's literary treasures, admiring the architectural splendor of Villa Necchi Campiglio, or discovering the artistic wonders of

San Bernardino alle Ossa, these off-the-beaten-path attractions beckon visitors to embark on a journey of discovery amidst the vibrant tapestry of Milan.

4.3 Museums and Art Galleries

Milan, the vibrant metropolis in northern Italy, is not only renowned for its fashion and design but also boasts a rich cultural heritage. Among its numerous attractions, the city's museums and art galleries stand out as must-visit destinations for any traveler seeking to delve into Milan's history, art, and culture. In this essay, we will take an extensive journey through six of Milan's most notable museums and art galleries, exploring their locations, significance, and why they are worth experiencing firsthand.

Pinacoteca di Brera

Nestled in the heart of Milan's historic center, the Pinacoteca di Brera is a treasure trove of Italian art spanning from the Middle Ages to the 20th century. Located in the Palazzo Brera, this renowned art gallery showcases masterpieces by Italian artists such as Raphael, Caravaggio, and Mantegna, among others. Visitors can immerse themselves in the captivating works of art while admiring the stunning architecture of the palazzo itself. To reach the Pinacoteca di Brera, one can easily take the metro to the Lanza station or opt for a leisurely stroll through Milan's charming streets. The entry fee is typically modest, offering excellent value for the experience it provides. Beyond its impressive collection, the Pinacoteca di Brera offers visitors a glimpse into Italy's rich artistic heritage, providing insight into the evolution of artistic styles over the centuries. Moreover, the tranquil atmosphere within the gallery allows for contemplation and appreciation of the artworks in a serene setting.

Museo del Novecento

Situated in the Palazzo dell'Arengario overlooking the Piazza del Duomo, the Museo del Novecento offers a captivating journey through 20th-century Italian art. This museum houses an extensive collection of paintings, sculptures, and installations by renowned artists such as Boccioni, Fontana, and Morandi, providing visitors with a comprehensive overview of Italy's artistic contributions to the modern era. Accessible via the Duomo metro station, the Museo del Novecento is conveniently located in the heart of Milan's historic district. The Museo del Novecento serves as a testament to Italy's cultural vitality during the tumultuous 20th century, offering visitors a deeper understanding of the artistic movements that shaped the nation's identity. Additionally, the museum's strategic location allows for easy exploration of other nearby attractions, making it an ideal starting point for a day of cultural enrichment in Milan.

Leonardo da Vinci National Museum of Science and Technology

Dedicated to the life and works of the Renaissance polymath Leonardo da Vinci, this museum is a celebration of innovation and ingenuity. Located in the historic monastery of San Vittore al Corpo, the Leonardo da Vinci National Museum of Science and Technology houses an extensive collection of Leonardo's inventions, scientific models, and artworks, providing visitors with a fascinating glimpse into the mind of one of history's greatest geniuses. Accessible via the Sant'Ambrogio metro station, the museum offers a unique blend of history, art, and science in one captivating setting. Beyond its historical significance, the museum offers interactive exhibits and workshops that appeal to visitors of all ages, making it a perfect destination for families and curious minds alike. Moreover, the museum's emphasis on Leonardo's contributions to science and technology underscores Milan's role as a hub of innovation throughout history.

Galleria d'Arte Moderna

Housed in the neoclassical Villa Reale, the Galleria d'Arte Moderna showcases an impressive collection of 19th and 20th-century Italian art, including works by renowned artists such as Modigliani, Boccioni, and Canova. Located in the lush surroundings of Milan's Indro Montanelli Public Gardens, the museum offers a peaceful retreat from the bustling city streets. Accessible via the Palestro metro station, the Galleria d'Arte Moderna is a hidden gem waiting to be discovered by art enthusiasts and nature lovers alike. In addition to its exceptional collection, the museum's tranquil setting provides the perfect backdrop for contemplation and reflection, allowing visitors to immerse themselves fully in the beauty of Italian art. Moreover, the Galleria d'Arte Moderna offers temporary exhibitions and cultural events that ensure there is always something new to discover with each visit.

Museum of the Sforza Castle

Located within the historic confines of the Sforza Castle, this museum offers a fascinating journey through Milan's storied past. From medieval armor and weaponry to Renaissance sculptures and decorative arts, the Museum of the Sforza Castle provides insight into the city's tumultuous history and cultural heritage. Accessible via the Cairoli metro station, the museum is conveniently situated near other notable landmarks such as the Duomo and the Teatro alla Scala, making it an essential stop for any visitor to Milan. Beyond its impressive collection, the museum offers visitors the opportunity to explore the majestic Sforza Castle itself, providing a glimpse into Milan's Renaissance splendor. Additionally, the museum's diverse exhibits cater to a wide range of interests, ensuring there is something for everyone to enjoy.

Milan's museums and art galleries provide a captivating exploration of the city's abundant cultural heritage, providing visitors with insight into its artistic legacy and historical significance. Whether exploring the masterpieces of the Pinacoteca di Brera, marveling at Leonardo da Vinci's inventions, or immersing oneself in the tranquility of the Galleria d'Arte Moderna, these institutions offer a wealth of experiences waiting to be discovered. From the heart of the historic center to the lush surroundings of public gardens, Milan's cultural treasures await those eager to explore its vibrant past and dynamic present.

4.4 Parks and Green Spaces

Milan, renowned for its fashion, culture, and history, also boasts a collection of splendid parks and green spaces that offer a tranquil escape from the bustling city life. These verdant havens not only provide a breath of fresh air but also serve as cultural landmarks steeped in history and significance. Here, we delve into six must-visit parks and green spaces in Milan, each offering a unique experience and allure.

Parco Sempione: A Green Oasis in the Heart of Milan

Located in the center of Milan, Parco Sempione is an extensive urban park that spans over 38 hectares. Located adjacent to the Sforza Castle, this picturesque park is easily accessible from the city center. Visitors can reach Parco Sempione by various means of public transportation, including tram, bus, or metro. One of the remarkable features of Parco Sempione is its free admission, welcoming visitors from all walks of life to explore its lush landscapes and iconic landmarks. Steeped in historical significance, the park was designed in the late 19th century by architect Emilio Alemagna, offering a harmonious blend of natural beauty and architectural splendor.

Upon arrival, visitors are greeted by the majestic Arco della Pace (Arch of Peace), a neoclassical triumphal arch that serves as the park's entrance. As visitors meander through the park's winding paths and verdant lawns, they encounter an array of attractions, including the peaceful Sempione Park Lake, where paddleboats are available for leisurely rides.

Giardini Pubblici Indro Montanelli: A Tranquil Retreat in Milan's Historic Center

Situated in the heart of Milan's historic center, Giardini Pubblici Indro Montanelli offers a serene retreat amidst the urban landscape. Named after the renowned Italian journalist and historian, this enchanting park spans approximately 17 acres and is easily accessible by public transportation.

Entrance to Giardini Pubblici Indro Montanelli is free of charge, making it an ideal destination for budget-conscious travelers seeking respite from the city's hustle and bustle. The park's origins date back to the 18th century when it was initially designed as a botanical garden. Today, it serves as a cultural hub, hosting outdoor concerts, art exhibitions, and recreational activities throughout the year. As visitors stroll through the park's manicured gardens and shaded pathways, they encounter notable landmarks such as the Natural History Museum and the iconic Planetarium. Additionally, the park features playgrounds for children, making it a popular destination for families seeking outdoor recreation.

Parco Lambro: A Natural Haven on Milan's Outskirts

For those seeking a tranquil escape from the urban sprawl, Parco Lambro offers a peaceful retreat on the outskirts of Milan. Located in the eastern part of the city, this expansive park spans over 240 hectares and is easily accessible by public transportation or car. Entry to Parco Lambro is free of charge, allowing visitors to immerse themselves in the park's natural beauty without any financial constraints. Originally established in the 1930s, the park encompasses diverse ecosystems, including woodlands, meadows, and wetlands, providing a habitat for a variety of plant and animal species. Parco Lambro holds cultural significance as a testament to Milan's commitment to environmental conservation and sustainable urban development. Guests can partake in a plethora of outdoor activities, including hiking, cycling, and birdwatching, amidst the park's picturesque landscapes. Additionally, the park offers picnic areas and barbecue facilities, making it an ideal destination for a day of leisure with family and friends.

Parco Nord Milano: A Recreational Haven for Outdoor Enthusiasts

Spanning over 600 hectares, Parco Nord Milano is one of the largest urban parks in Europe, offering an expansive playground for outdoor enthusiasts. Located in the northern outskirts of Milan, this sprawling green space is easily accessible by public transportation, with several entrances throughout the park. Entry to Parco Nord Milano is free of charge, inviting visitors to explore its vast expanse of meadows, woodlands, and waterways. Established in the 1970s, the park serves as a recreational haven, boasting a wide range of facilities and amenities for visitors of all ages. Whether indulging in a leisurely bike ride along the park's extensive network of cycling trails or enjoying a picnic amidst the tranquil surroundings, there's something for everyone at Parco Nord Milano. The park also features sports fields, playgrounds, and fitness circuits, catering to fitness enthusiasts and families alike.

Parco delle Cave: A Nature Reserve Amidst Urban Landscapes

Parco delle Cave offers a unique blend of natural beauty and industrial heritage. Located in the western part of the city, this captivating nature reserve spans over 70 hectares and is easily accessible by public transportation or car. Entry to Parco delle Cave is free of charge, allowing visitors to explore its diverse ecosystems and rehabilitated quarry sites. Originally used for the extraction of sand and gravel, the park has been transformed into a haven for biodiversity, featuring wetlands, meadows, and woodland habitats.

Parco delle Cave holds cultural significance as a symbol of environmental restoration and sustainable land use practices. Visitors can embark on guided nature walks, birdwatching expeditions, or cycling adventures, immersing themselves in the park's natural wonders. Additionally, the park offers educational programs and workshops for visitors interested in learning about conservation efforts and ecological restoration.

Orto Botanico di Brera: A Botanical Gem in Milan's Artistic Quarter

Tucked away in Milan's artistic quarter, Orto Botanico di Brera is a hidden gem waiting to be discovered by plant enthusiasts and nature lovers alike. Located near the renowned Brera Art Gallery, this enchanting botanical garden spans approximately 5,000 square meters and is easily accessible by public transportation. Entry to Orto Botanico di Brera is typically free or requires a nominal fee, making it an accessible destination for visitors of all ages. Established in the late 18th century, the botanical garden boasts a diverse collection of plant species, including exotic specimens from around the world. Visitors to Orto Botanico di Brera can wander through its tranquil pathways, marveling at rare plants, fragrant flowers, and towering trees. The garden also features historic greenhouses, where visitors can explore tropical and subtropical ecosystems. Additionally, the botanical garden hosts educational events, botanical art exhibitions, and guided tours, offering visitors a deeper understanding of plant biodiversity and conservation.

Milan's parks and green spaces offer a wealth of opportunities for exploration, relaxation, and cultural enrichment. Whether it's strolling through the manicured gardens of Parco Sempione, cycling along the scenic trails of Parco Nord Milano, or immersing oneself in the botanical wonders of Orto Botanico di Brera, there's something for every visitor to enjoy. With their rich history, cultural significance, and diverse landscapes, these green oases beckon travelers to embark on a journey of discovery amidst the vibrant tapestry of Milan.

4.5 Architectural Marvels and Modern Landmarks

Milan, often recognized as the fashion and financial capital of Italy, is also a city steeped in history and architectural grandeur. Beyond its renowned fashion boutiques and bustling streets, Milan boasts an array of architectural marvels and modern landmarks that captivate visitors from around the world. These sites not only showcase the city's rich history but also its innovative contemporary spirit. Let's delve into six of Milan's most notable architectural wonders and modern landmarks that are essential stops for any visitor.

Milan Cathedral (Duomo di Milano)

Located at the heart of Milan, the Duomo di Milano is a magnificent Gothic cathedral that stands as one of the largest churches in the world. Its intricate façade adorned with spires, statues, and countless marble details is a sight to behold. Visitors can marvel at the cathedral's impressive architecture, ascend to the rooftop for panoramic views of the city, or explore its ornate interior filled with stunning stained glass windows and intricate sculptures. To reach the Duomo, visitors can easily take the metro to the Duomo station, which is located nearby. The cathedral is open to visitors daily, with varying hours depending on religious services and events. While entry to the cathedral is free, there is a fee to access the rooftop terraces and the museum. The Duomo di Milano holds immense cultural and historical significance, serving as a symbol of Milan's religious devotion and architectural prowess. A visit to this iconic landmark offers a glimpse into the city's medieval past and provides unparalleled views of Milan's skyline.

Galleria Vittorio Emanuele II

Adjacent to the Duomo, the Galleria Vittorio Emanuele II is an exquisite 19th-century shopping arcade renowned for its stunning architecture and luxury boutiques. Designed by architect Giuseppe Mengoni, the Galleria is a masterpiece of glass and iron, featuring a magnificent glass dome and intricately decorated interiors. Visitors can stroll through the arcade, admire its elegant shops, and marvel at the mosaic floors depicting the emblems of Italy's major cities. The Galleria is not only a shopping destination but also a cultural hub, housing cafes, restaurants, and even a renowned bookstore. Located in the heart of Milan's historic center, the Galleria is easily accessible by foot from the Duomo or via public transportation. There is no entry fee to visit the Galleria Vittorio Emanuele II, making it an ideal spot for leisurely exploration. Whether indulging in retail therapy or simply admiring its architectural splendor, a visit to this iconic landmark is a must for any visitor to Milan.

Sforza Castle (Castello Sforzesco)

Situated in the heart of Milan, the Sforza Castle is a formidable fortress that has witnessed centuries of history. Originally built in the 15th century by the Duke of Milan, the castle underwent various transformations over the years and now houses several museums and art collections. Visitors can explore the castle grounds, which encompass lush gardens, courtyards, and defensive walls. Inside, they can visit museums such as the Museum of Ancient Art, the Museum of Musical Instruments, and the Michelangelo Gallery, which showcases the master's unfinished masterpiece, the Pietà Rondanini.

To reach the Sforza Castle, visitors can take the metro to the Cairoli or Cadorna station, both of which are within walking distance of the castle. While entry to the castle grounds is free, there may be a fee to access certain museums and exhibitions. The Sforza Castle is not only a historical landmark but also a cultural hub, offering visitors a glimpse into Milan's rich artistic heritage.

Bosco Verticale

A striking example of modern architecture, the Bosco Verticale, or Vertical Forest, is a pair of residential towers located in Milan's Porta Nuova district. Designed by architect Stefano Boeri, these innovative skyscrapers are covered in lush greenery, creating a vertical forest in the heart of the city. Visitors can marvel at the towers' unique design, which not only enhances the cityscape but also promotes sustainability and biodiversity. The Bosco Verticale serves as a model for urban green spaces, offering residents a high-quality living environment while mitigating the effects of urbanization.

To reach the Bosco Verticale, visitors can take the metro to the Garibaldi station, which is a short walk from the towers. While access to the residential units is restricted, visitors can admire the towers from the street level and appreciate their contribution to Milan's architectural landscape. The Bosco Verticale is a symbol of the city's commitment to innovation and environmental stewardship, making it a must-see attraction for architecture enthusiasts and nature lovers alike.

Fondazione Prada

Located in a former distillery in Milan's southern outskirts, the Fondazione Prada is a contemporary art complex that seamlessly blends historic industrial architecture with modern design. Founded by the renowned fashion house Prada, the foundation showcases a diverse range of contemporary art exhibitions, installations, and cultural events. Visitors can explore the foundation's sprawling campus, which includes exhibition spaces, a cinema, a library, and a café designed by filmmaker Wes Anderson. The complex also features striking architectural elements, including a golden tower designed by Rem Koolhaas and a courtyard adorned with sculptures by Louise Bourgeois.

To reach the Fondazione Prada, visitors can take public transportation to the Lodi T.I.B.B. station, which is a short walk from the complex. While there is an entry fee to access certain exhibitions and events, the foundation also offers free admission to its permanent collection and outdoor spaces. The Fondazione Prada is not only a cultural institution but also a testament to Milan's dynamic arts scene and commitment to creativity.

CityLife

CityLife is a modern urban redevelopment project located in the heart of Milan, encompassing residential, commercial, and recreational spaces. Anchored by three iconic skyscrapers designed by renowned architects Zaha Hadid, Arata Isozaki, and Daniel Libeskind, CityLife represents the future of urban living in Milan. Visitors can explore the sprawling complex, which includes shopping centers, restaurants, parks, and cultural venues. They can also admire the striking architecture of the skyscrapers, which redefine Milan's skyline with their innovative design and futuristic aesthetics.

To reach CityLife, visitors can take the metro to the Tre Torri station, which is located adjacent to the complex. Entry to CityLife is free, allowing visitors to stroll through its pedestrian-friendly streets and enjoy its vibrant atmosphere. Whether shopping, dining, or simply soaking in the modern ambiance, CityLife offers a glimpse into Milan's evolving urban landscape and its vision for the future.

Milan's architectural marvels and modern landmarks represent the city's rich tapestry of history, innovation, and creativity. From centuries-old cathedrals to cutting-edge skyscrapers, these iconic sites offer visitors a diverse range of experiences that showcase Milan's past, present, and future. Whether exploring medieval fortresses, wandering through contemporary art galleries, or marveling at vertical forests, a visit to Milan's architectural wonders is sure to leave a lasting impression on any traveler. With its blend of tradition and modernity, Milan truly stands as a must-see destination for architecture enthusiasts, cultural aficionados, and curious explorers alike.

CHAPTER 5

PRACTICAL INFORMATION AND TRAVEL RESOURCES

5.1 Maps and Navigation

Click the link or Scan the QR Code with a device to view a comprehensive map of Milan – https://shorturl.at/lCRX1

Exploring the vibrant city of Milan is an exciting endeavor, filled with cultural delights, historical landmarks, and culinary adventures. Whether you're wandering through the cobblestone streets of the historic center or marveling at the modern architecture of the city's skyscrapers, having reliable maps and navigation tools is essential for making the most of your visit. In this guide, we'll explore the various options for accessing maps in Milan, from traditional tourist maps to digital navigation apps.

Milan Tourist Map

One of the most convenient ways to navigate Milan's attractions is by using a traditional tourist map. These maps are readily available at tourist information centers, hotels, and museums throughout the city. A typical Milan tourist map highlights key landmarks, neighborhoods, and transportation routes, making it easy for visitors to plan their itinerary and navigate the city streets.

To obtain a tourist map in Milan, you can visit the city's main tourist information center, located near the Duomo, or inquire at your hotel's front desk. These maps are often free of charge and come with helpful tips and suggestions for sightseeing, dining, and shopping in Milan. They are especially useful for first-time visitors who may not be familiar with the city's layout and attractions.

Digital Maps

In today's digital age, navigating Milan has never been easier thanks to a plethora of digital mapping apps and websites. From Google Maps to Apple Maps, there are numerous options available for accessing detailed maps of Milan right at your fingertips. These digital maps offer real-time navigation, traffic updates, and public transportation information, making them invaluable tools for exploring the city efficiently.

To access digital maps in Milan, simply download a mapping app onto your smartphone or tablet before your trip. Apps like Google Maps and Apple Maps are user-friendly and offer offline functionality, allowing you to navigate even without an internet connection. Additionally, many public transportation systems in Milan have their own apps that provide real-time schedules and route information for buses, trams, and metro lines.

Accessing Maps Offline (Paper Map)

While digital maps are convenient, it's always a good idea to have a backup plan in case of technology glitches or battery drain. That's where offline paper maps come in handy. Before setting out to explore Milan, consider picking up a physical map from a tourist information center or purchasing one from a bookstore. These maps are durable, easy to carry, and don't require batteries or an internet connection. To access offline paper maps in Milan, visit the city's main tourist information center or look for map vendors at popular tourist attractions. Many hotels also provide complimentary maps to their guests upon request. Having a physical map on hand can be particularly useful for navigating narrow alleyways and hidden gems in Milan's historic neighborhoods.

Accessing Milan's Maps Digitally

For travelers who prefer the convenience of digital maps, accessing Milan's maps online is a breeze. In addition to popular mapping apps like Google Maps and Apple Maps, there are also dedicated websites and platforms that offer comprehensive maps of Milan. One such option is the official website of the Milan Tourism Board, which provides interactive maps, walking tours, and insider tips for exploring the city.

To access Milan's maps digitally, simply visit the Milan Tourism Board's website or search for Milan maps on your preferred search engine. Many tourist attractions and landmarks also have their own websites with detailed maps and directions for visitors. Additionally, consider using QR codes found in guidebooks or tourist brochures to quickly access digital maps on your smartphone or tablet.

Comprehensive Map of Milan

As an author of travel guides and an experienced traveler, I highly recommend clicking on the link or scanning the QR code provided in this book to view a comprehensive map of Milan. This interactive map will help you plan your itinerary, discover hidden gems, and navigate the city with ease. Whether you're exploring historic landmarks, shopping districts, or trendy neighborhoods, having a comprehensive map of Milan at your fingertips is essential for a memorable and stress-free experience.BNavigating Milan's bustling streets and diverse neighborhoods is made easy with a variety of mapping options at your disposal. Whether you prefer traditional paper maps or digital navigation apps, there are plenty of resources available to help you explore the city with confidence.

From iconic landmarks to hidden gems, having reliable maps and navigation tools will ensure that you make the most of your visit to Milan. So grab a map, plan your route, and get ready to embark on an unforgettable journey through this dynamic and vibrant city.

5.2 Essential Packing List

Packing for a trip to Milan, the bustling fashion and cultural capital of Italy, requires careful consideration to ensure you have everything you need for an enjoyable and comfortable stay. From exploring historic landmarks to indulging in gourmet cuisine and shopping in stylish boutiques, Milan offers a diverse array of experiences that warrant a well-thought-out packing list. In this guide, we'll cover the essential items you'll need to pack for your visit to Milan.

Clothing and Footwear

Milan's weather can vary depending on the season, so it's essential to pack clothing suitable for the time of year you'll be visiting. In general, lightweight and breathable clothing is ideal for the summer months, while layers and warmer attire are necessary for the cooler seasons. Don't forget to pack comfortable walking shoes, as you'll likely be exploring Milan's streets on foot, and a pair of dressier shoes for evenings out or visits to upscale establishments.

Travel Documents and Essentials

Before embarking on your journey to Milan, ensure you have all necessary travel documents and essentials on hand. This includes your passport, travel itinerary, airline tickets, hotel reservations, and any relevant visas or travel insurance documents. Additionally, consider carrying a copy of important documents such as your passport and emergency contact information in case of loss or theft.

Electronics and Gadgets

To capture memories of your trip to Milan and stay connected while abroad, be sure to pack essential electronics and gadgets. This may include your smartphone, camera, charger, adapter plug for European outlets, and any other devices you rely on for communication or entertainment. Don't forget to download offline maps and travel apps to assist with navigation and language translation.

Personal Care and Toiletries

While you can easily purchase toiletries and personal care items in Milan, it's a good idea to pack travel-sized essentials to have on hand upon arrival. This may include items such as toothpaste, shampoo, conditioner, sunscreen, insect repellent, and any prescription medications you require. Remember to adhere to airline regulations regarding liquids and gels in your carry-on luggage.

Travel Accessories

To enhance your travel experience and stay organized throughout your trip to Milan, consider packing a few essential travel accessories. This may include a lightweight backpack or daypack for sightseeing excursions, a reusable water bottle to stay hydrated, a travel umbrella or raincoat for unexpected showers, and a portable power bank to keep your devices charged while on the go.

Fashionable Attire

As one of the world's leading fashion capitals, Milan is synonymous with style and sophistication. When packing for your visit, be sure to include fashionable attire suitable for exploring the city's chic neighborhoods, dining at trendy restaurants, and attending cultural events. Consider packing a few versatile pieces that can easily transition from day to night, such as a classic blazer, stylish scarf, and statement accessories.

Cultural Considerations

While Milan is a cosmopolitan city with a diverse population, it's essential to respect local customs and cultural norms during your visit. This may include dressing modestly when visiting religious sites or conservative neighborhoods, covering your shoulders and knees, and removing your shoes before entering certain establishments. Additionally, familiarize yourself with basic Italian phrases and etiquette to communicate respectfully with locals.

Health and Safety Essentials

Prioritize your health and safety by packing essential items to ensure a smooth and worry-free trip to Milan. This may include a small first aid kit with bandages, pain relievers, and any necessary medications, as well as hand sanitizer and disinfectant wipes for maintaining hygiene while traveling. It's also wise to carry a copy of your health insurance information and emergency contact numbers in case of illness or injury.

Packing for a visit to Milan requires thoughtful consideration to ensure you have everything you need for a comfortable and enjoyable stay in this dynamic city. By packing essential items such as appropriate clothing, travel documents, electronics, personal care items, and travel accessories, you'll be well-prepared to explore Milan's historic landmarks, fashionable boutiques, and culinary delights with ease. Remember to respect local customs and cultural norms, prioritize your health and safety, and embrace the unique experiences that Milan has to offer. With careful planning and packing, your trip to Milan is sure to be a memorable and fulfilling experience.

5.3 Visa Requirements and Entry Procedures

Before planning your trip to Milan, it's essential to understand the visa requirements for your specific country of origin. Italy is a member of the Schengen Area, which allows for visa-free travel for citizens of many countries for short stays. However, visitors from certain countries may require a Schengen visa for entry. To determine whether you need a visa to visit Milan, check the official website of the Italian consulate or embassy in your home country. Visa requirements may vary depending on factors such as the purpose of your visit, the duration of your stay, and your nationality. Be sure to apply for your visa well in advance of your planned travel dates to allow for processing time.

Entry Procedures by Air Travel

For most international visitors, arriving in Milan by air is the most convenient and popular option. Milan is served by two main airports: Malpensa Airport (MXP) and Linate Airport (LIN). Malpensa Airport is the larger of the two and handles a significant portion of international flights, while Linate Airport primarily serves domestic and European destinations. Upon arrival at Malpensa or Linate Airport, travelers will go through immigration and customs procedures. If you're traveling from a Schengen Area country, you'll go through immigration controls upon arrival, where your passport will be stamped. For travelers from non-Schengen countries, you may need to present your visa and complete a customs declaration form.

Entry Procedures by Train

Traveling to Milan by train is another popular option, especially for visitors coming from other European cities. Milan is well-connected to major European cities via high-speed rail networks such as the Eurostar Italia and Thello trains. The city's main train station, Milano Centrale, is one of the largest and busiest in Europe, offering domestic and international services. Upon arrival at Milano Centrale or other train stations in Milan, travelers will typically go through ticket and passport control if arriving from another country. For travelers within the Schengen Area, there are usually no passport checks when traveling by train between member countries. However, it's essential to have your passport or ID card with you for identification purposes.

Entry Procedures by Road

If you're traveling to Milan by road from another European country, you'll likely cross the border without formal passport controls if both countries are part of the Schengen Area. However, it's always a good idea to carry your passport or ID card with you for identification purposes. If you're arriving in Milan by car from a non-Schengen country, you may encounter border controls and customs checks at the border crossing. Be prepared to present your passport, visa (if required), vehicle registration, and insurance documents. It's also essential to familiarize yourself with the driving regulations and requirements in Italy, including road signage, speed limits, and toll fees.

Airlines and Booking Procedures

When it comes to booking flights to Milan, there are several airlines that offer direct and connecting flights from major cities around the world. Here are six airlines commonly used for traveling to Milan:

Alitalia: Italy's national airline, offering direct flights to Milan from major cities worldwide. Website: (https://www.alitalia.com/)

Lufthansa: A leading German airline with extensive connectivity to Milan from Europe and beyond. Website: (https://www.lufthansa.com/)

Emirates: Dubai-based airline offering connecting flights to Milan from various destinations in the Middle East, Asia, and beyond. Website: (https://www.emirates.com/)

British Airways: UK's flag carrier airline offering direct flights to Milan from London and connecting flights from other major cities. Website:(https://www.britishairways.com/)

Air France: French airline offering connecting flights to Milan from Paris and other major European cities. Website:(https://www.airfrance.com/)

Delta Air Lines: US-based airline offering connecting flights to Milan from North America and other international destinations. Website: (https://www.delta.com/)

To book flights with these airlines, you can visit their official websites or use online travel agencies and booking platforms. It's advisable to compare prices and flight options to find the best deals and travel times for your itinerary. Planning your visit to Milan involves understanding the visa requirements and entry procedures, whether you're arriving by air, train, or road. Be sure to check visa requirements well in advance and prepare all necessary documents for entry. Arriving in Milan by air offers convenient access through the city's main airports, while traveling by train or road provides alternative options for visitors coming from other European destinations. When booking flights, consider airlines such as Alitalia, Lufthansa, Emirates, British Airways, Air France, and Delta Air Lines, which offer extensive connectivity to Milan from major cities worldwide. With careful planning and preparation, your journey to Milan is sure to be a smooth and memorable experience.

5.4 Safety Tips and Emergency Contacts

Ensuring your safety during your visit to Milan is paramount to enjoying a stress-free and memorable experience in the city. While Milan is generally considered safe for tourists, it's essential to take precautions and be prepared for any emergencies that may arise. By following safety tips and knowing emergency contacts, you can navigate Milan with confidence and peace of mind.

Safety Tips

Stay Vigilant: Like any major city, Milan has its share of petty crimes such as pickpocketing and theft. Keep an eye on your belongings, especially in crowded tourist areas, public transportation, and busy markets. Use a secure crossbody bag or money belt to keep your valuables close to you.

Be Aware of Scams: Beware of common scams targeting tourists, such as fake petitions, distraction techniques, and overcharging at restaurants or taxis. If something seems suspicious or too good to be true, trust your instincts and walk away.

Stay in Well-Lit Areas: When exploring Milan at night, stick to well-lit streets and avoid isolated areas, particularly in less touristy neighborhoods. Travel in groups whenever possible and avoid walking alone late at night.

Know Your Surroundings: Familiarize yourself with the layout of Milan's streets, neighborhoods, and public transportation routes. Carry a map or use a navigation app on your smartphone to avoid getting lost, especially in unfamiliar areas.

Respect Local Customs: Milan is a diverse and cosmopolitan city, but it's essential to respect local customs and cultural norms. Dress modestly when visiting religious sites, be mindful of noise levels in residential areas, and follow posted rules and regulations.

Emergency Preparedness: Be prepared for emergencies by carrying a charged cell phone with emergency contacts programmed in, including local police, ambulance, and fire department numbers. Additionally, know the location of the nearest hospitals and medical facilities in case of injury or illness.

Emergency Contacts

Police (Carabinieri): To report emergencies or criminal incidents, dial 112 for the Carabinieri, Italy's national military police force. The Carabinieri are responsible for law enforcement and public safety throughout the country, including Milan.

Ambulance (Ambulanza): In case of medical emergencies or accidents, dial 118 to request an ambulance. Emergency medical services in Milan are coordinated by the local health authorities and dispatched promptly to provide assistance.

Fire Department (Vigili del Fuoco): For fires, rescue operations, or other emergencies requiring the assistance of the fire department, dial 115. The Vigili del Fuoco are responsible for firefighting, rescue services, and disaster response in Milan and across Italy.

Tourist Police (Polizia Municipale): The Tourist Police in Milan provide assistance and support to visitors, including help with lost belongings, tourist information, and safety tips. They can be reached by dialing 113.

Consular Assistance: If you are a foreign national in need of consular assistance, contact your country's embassy or consulate in Milan. They can provide support with passport issues, legal assistance, and other consular services.

Additional Safety Tips

Travel Insurance: Consider purchasing travel insurance before your trip to Milan to cover unexpected emergencies, medical expenses, and trip cancellations.

Stay Connected: Keep in touch with family and friends back home by sharing your itinerary, checking in regularly, and letting them know how to reach you in case of emergency.

Stay Informed: Stay updated on local news, weather forecasts, and any safety advisories or alerts that may affect your travel plans while in Milan.

By following safety tips, staying informed, and knowing emergency contacts, you can ensure a safe and enjoyable visit to Milan. While the city offers a wealth of cultural attractions, culinary delights, and historic landmarks to explore, it's essential to prioritize your safety and be prepared for any unforeseen circumstances. With proper planning and precautions, you can make the most of your time in Milan and create lasting memories in this vibrant Italian metropolis.

5.5 Currency, Banking, Budgeting and Money Matters

Before embarking on your journey to Milan, it's essential to familiarize yourself with the local currency and banking options available to you during your stay. Italy's official currency is the Euro (EUR), which is used throughout the country, including Milan. While major credit cards are widely accepted in hotels, restaurants, and larger establishments, it'sIt's always advisable to carry some cash for smaller purchases and transactions.

Currency Exchange

Upon arrival in Milan, you'll find numerous currency exchange offices (bureaux de change) located throughout the city, particularly in tourist areas and transportation hubs such as airports and train stations. These exchange offices offer competitive rates for converting foreign currency into euros. Be sure to compare rates and fees before making an exchange, and avoid exchanging money at airports or tourist hotspots where rates may be less favorable.

Banking Services

Milan is home to several banks and financial institutions that offer a range of services for visitors, including currency exchange, ATM withdrawals, and international money transfers. Key banking institutions in Milan comprise UniCredit, Intesa Sanpaolo, Banca Popolare di Milano, Banco BPM, Monte dei Paschi di Siena, and Cassa Depositi e Prestiti.

Special Services for Visitors

Many banks in Milan offer special services tailored to the needs of international visitors. These services may include multi-currency accounts, foreign currency savings accounts, and international debit/credit cards with no foreign transaction fees. Additionally, some banks provide assistance in English and other languages to help visitors navigate their banking needs more easily.

ATM Acces

ATMs (bancomats) are readily available throughout Milan, allowing visitors to withdraw euros using their debit or credit cards. ATMs can be found in bank branches, shopping centers, and other public spaces. It's essential to check with your home bank regarding any fees or charges for using ATMs abroad, as well as to inform them of your travel plans to avoid potential issues with card authorization.

Budgeting Tips

Milan is known for its high-end fashion, luxury dining, and upscale accommodations, but it's also possible to explore the city on a budget. Here are some budgeting tips for visitors to Milan:

Accommodation: Consider staying in budget-friendly accommodations such as hostels, guesthouses, or Airbnb rentals in less central neighborhoods to save on accommodation costs.

Transportation: Use public transportation such as buses and metro trains to get around the city affordably. Consider purchasing a multi-day transportation pass for unlimited travel during your stay.

Dining: Look for local trattorias, cafes, and street food vendors for affordable dining options. Avoid dining in touristy areas, where prices tend to be higher.

Attractions: Many of Milan's top attractions, such as the Duomo di Milano and Sforza Castle, offer free or discounted admission on certain days or with city passes. Plan your visits accordingly to save on entrance fees.

Shopping: While Milan is famous for its fashion and shopping, you can still find bargains at outlet stores, flea markets, and discount shops throughout the city. Set a budget for shopping and stick to it to avoid overspending.

Bureau de Change Locations

For visitors in need of currency exchange services, there are several reputable bureau de change locations in Milan. Some of the well-known exchange offices include ChangeGroup, Forexchange, Global Blue, and Travelex. These offices are typically located in central areas such as Piazza del Duomo, Milan Central Station, and popular shopping district. Navigating currency, banking, budgeting, and other money matters during your visit to Milan is essential for a smooth and enjoyable experience. Familiarize yourself with the local currency, banking options, and budgeting tips to make the most of your time in the city. Whether you're exchanging currency, withdrawing cash from ATMs, or sticking to a budget while exploring Milan's attractions and dining scene, proper planning and preparation will ensure a stress-free and memorable visit to this vibrant Italian metropolis.

5.6 Language, Communication and Useful Phrases

Italian serves as the official language spoken in Milan and across Italy. While English is widely understood in tourist areas and among younger generations, especially in major cities like Milan, it's always appreciated to make an effort to communicate in Italian. Learning a few basic Italian phrases can enhance your travel experience and help you connect with locals on a deeper level.

Useful Phrases

Here are some useful Italian phrases and expressions to help you navigate Milan with ease:

- *Buongiorno: Good morning*
- *Buonasera: Good evening*
- *Buon giorno: Good day*
- *Ciao: Hello/goodbye (informal)*
- *Grazie: Thank you*
- *Prego: You're welcome*
- *Per favore: Please*
- *Mi scusi: Excuse me*
- *Parla inglese?: Do you speak English?*
- *Posso avere il conto, per favore?: Can I have the bill, please?*
- *Dove si trova il bagno?: Where is the bathroom?*
- *Quanto costa?: How much does it cost?*
- *Mi chiamo [Your Name]: My name is [Your Name]*
- *Non parlo italiano molto bene: I don't speak Italian very well*

Communication Tips

While many Milanese residents speak English, especially in tourist areas, it's polite to greet people in Italian and attempt to communicate in the local language whenever possible. Speaking slowly and clearly, using simple phrases, and using hand gestures can help facilitate communication, even if you're not fluent in Italian. If you encounter a language barrier, don't be afraid to use translation apps on your smartphone or carry a pocket dictionary to help you communicate. Locals will appreciate your effort to communicate in their language, even if it's just a few basic phrases.

Language Schools and Courses

For visitors interested in learning Italian or improving their language skills during their stay in Milan, there are several language schools and courses available throughout the city. These schools offer a range of programs, from intensive courses for beginners to conversation classes for more advanced learners. Some well-known language schools in Milan include Scuola Leonardo da Vinci, International House Milan, and Centro Italiano.

Multilingual Services

In addition to Italian and English, Milan is a multicultural city with residents from around the world, so you may encounter people who speak other languages as well. Many hotels, restaurants, and tourist attractions offer multilingual services and have staff members who speak languages such as Spanish, French, German, and Chinese to accommodate diverse visitors.

Language and communication play a vital role in enhancing your travel experience in Milan. While Italian is the official language spoken in the city, English is widely understood, especially in tourist areas. Learning a few basic Italian phrases can help you navigate Milan with ease and connect with locals on a more personal level. Don't hesitate to make an effort to communicate in Italian, use translation tools when needed, and take advantage of language schools and multilingual services to enrich your experience in this vibrant Italian metropolis.

5.7 Useful Websites, Mobile Apps and Online Resources

Planning a visit to Milan can be made much more convenient and enjoyable with the help of various websites, mobile apps, and online resources tailored to travelers' needs. Whether you're looking for information on attractions, transportation, dining, or accommodations, there are numerous digital tools available to assist you in navigating the city and making the most of your trip.

VisitMilano

VisitMilano is the official tourism website for the city of Milan, offering comprehensive information on attractions, events, accommodations, dining, and transportation options. The website features interactive maps, suggested itineraries, and practical tips for visitors. Additionally, VisitMilano provides updates on special events, exhibitions, and cultural happenings in the city, allowing travelers to plan their itinerary accordingly.

TripAdvisor

TripAdvisor is a popular travel planning platform that provides reviews, recommendations, and ratings for hotels, restaurants, attractions, and activities in Milan. Travelers can use the website or mobile app to research and book accommodations, read user reviews, and discover hidden gems recommended by fellow travelers. TripAdvisor also offers booking options for tours, experiences, and transportation services in Milan.

Google Maps

Google Maps is an essential navigation tool for travelers, offering detailed maps, real-time traffic updates, and directions for exploring Milan. The mobile app allows users to search for nearby attractions, restaurants, and points of interest, as well as plan routes using public transportation options such as buses, trams, and metro trains. Google Maps also provides street view imagery and user-generated reviews to help travelers navigate the city with ease.

Milan Metro

The Milan Metro app is a handy tool for navigating Milan's extensive metro system, which consists of four lines serving the city and surrounding areas. The app provides real-time updates on train schedules, service disruptions, and station information, allowing travelers to plan their journeys and navigate the metro network efficiently. Additionally, the Milan Metro app offers offline functionality, making it ideal for use during your visit to Milan.

Eatwith

Eatwith is a unique dining platform that connects travelers with local hosts for authentic culinary experiences in Milan and other cities around the world. Through the Eatwith website or mobile app, travelers can discover and book meals hosted by Milanese chefs and home cooks, offering opportunities to enjoy homemade Italian cuisine and immerse themselves in the local food culture. Eatwith experiences range from cooking classes and food tours to intimate dinner parties and wine tastings.

Citymapper
Citymapper is a comprehensive transportation app that provides detailed route planning and navigation for public transit systems in cities around the world, including Milan. Travelers can use the app to find the fastest and most efficient routes using buses, trams, metro trains, and other modes of transportation in Milan. Citymapper also offers real-time updates on service disruptions, estimated travel times, and alternative routes, making it an invaluable tool for getting around the city.

Utilizing useful websites, mobile apps, and online resources can greatly enhance your travel experience in Milan, providing valuable information, navigation assistance, and booking options at your fingertips. Whether you're researching attractions, planning transportation routes, or seeking authentic dining experiences, there are digital tools available to cater to your needs and preferences. By leveraging these resources, you can make the most of your visit to Milan and create unforgettable memories in this vibrant Italian metropolis.

5.8 Visitor Centers and Tourist Assistance

When traversing the enchanting streets of Milan, it's beneficial to know about the myriad of visitor centers and tourist assistance available to make your exploration seamless and enriching. Whether you're seeking guidance on must-see attractions, cultural events, or practical information, these centers are dedicated to ensuring your visit to Milan is nothing short of exceptional.

MilanoTourism Visitor Center:
Location: Piazza Duomo, 14, 20122 Milano MI, Italy
Contact: +39 02 86918889
Website: www.turismo.milano.it

Located in the heart of the city, MilanoTourism Visitor Center serves as a hub for tourists eager to delve into Milan's rich tapestry of history and culture. Knowledgeable staff members are on hand to offer personalized recommendations, maps, and brochures, helping visitors craft bespoke itineraries tailored to their interests. From obtaining museum tickets to arranging guided tours, this center caters to all your travel needs.

ATM Point - Milano Cadorna:

Location: Piazza Cadorna, 20123 Milano MI, Italy

Contact: +39 02 48603535

Website: www.atm.it

Situated near Cadorna Railway Station, ATM Point provides comprehensive assistance to travelers navigating Milan's public transportation network. Visitors can obtain information on metro lines, tram routes, and bus schedules, facilitating seamless mobility throughout the city. Additionally, multilingual staff members offer insights into Milan's top attractions, dining hotspots, and shopping districts, ensuring an immersive and hassle-free experience for tourists.

Tourist Information Point - Milano Centrale:

Location: Stazione Centrale, Piazza Duca D'Aosta, 1, 20124 Milano MI, Italy

Contact: +39 02 66986790

Website: www.grandistazioni.it

Nestled within Milano Centrale Railway Station, Tourist Information Point caters to travelers arriving in Milan via train, providing indispensable guidance and support. From hotel reservations to transportation advice, this center offers a range of services to enhance your visit. Additionally, visitors can procure city maps, event calendars, and cultural insights, empowering them to immerse themselves fully in Milan's vibrant ambiance from the moment they step off the train.

Milan Visitor Center - Via Marconi:

Location: Via Marconi, 1, 20123 Milano MI, Italy

Contact: +39 02 85460756

Website: www.milanocastello.it

Tucked away in the vicinity of Sforza Castle, Milan Visitor Center serves as a beacon for travelers eager to uncover the city's hidden gems and historical landmarks. Friendly staff members offer insider tips on lesser-known attractions, walking tours, and culinary delights, enriching your Milanese experience with authentic local flavor. Whether you're seeking advice on navigating the city or recommendations for off-the-beaten-path excursions, this center is your gateway to Milan's multifaceted charm.

Milan Tourism Office - Linate Airport:
Location: Milan Linate Airport, Viale Enrico Forlanini, 20090 Segrate MI, Italy

Conveniently situated within Milan Linate Airport, Milan Tourism Office provides a warm welcome to travelers arriving in the city by air. Staffed by knowledgeable professionals, this office offers invaluable assistance ranging from transportation options to hotel accommodations, ensuring a smooth transition for visitors venturing into Milan. With a wealth of resources at your disposal, including city guides, event brochures, and transportation maps, you'll be well-equipped to embark on your Milanese odyssey with confidence and ease.

Whether you're a first-time visitor or a seasoned traveler returning to Milan's captivating embrace, these visitor centers and tourist assistance points stand ready to enhance your journey with unparalleled support and guidance. From practical advice to cultural insights, they embody the spirit of hospitality that defines Milan as a premier destination for exploration and discovery.

CHAPTER 6
CULINARY DELIGHTS

6.1 Traditional Milanese Cuisine

Milanese cuisine is characterized by its simplicity, reliance on high-quality ingredients, and emphasis on hearty flavors. Influenced by Lombardy's agricultural abundance and historical trade routes, traditional Milanese dishes often feature ingredients such as rice, polenta, saffron, and butter, along with locally sourced meats and cheeses. From iconic risotto dishes to indulgent desserts, Milanese cuisine offers a diverse array of flavors and textures that satisfy the palate and evoke a sense of culinary nostalgia.

Risotto alla Milanese

One of Milan's most iconic dishes, Risotto alla Milanese, is a creamy and aromatic rice dish flavored with saffron, butter, and Parmesan cheese. This luxurious dish is often served as a primo (first course) in Milanese trattorias and osterias, where it pairs perfectly with a glass of crisp Lombard white wine. Visitors can savor authentic Risotto alla Milanese at traditional restaurants throughout the city, with prices typically ranging from €10 to €20 per serving.

Cotoletta alla Milanese

Cotoletta alla Milanese is a classic Milanese dish consisting of a breaded and fried veal cutlet, traditionally served bone-in and accompanied by a wedge of lemon. This beloved dish is a staple of Milanese cuisine, with its origins dating back to the 19th century. Visitors can enjoy Cotoletta alla Milanese at local trattorias and ristorantes, where it is often served with a side of creamy mashed potatoes or a fresh salad. Prices for Cotoletta alla Milanese typically range from €15 to €30, depending on the restaurant and portion size.

Panettone

No visit to Milan is complete without indulging in a slice of Panettone, a traditional Italian Christmas cake hailing from Milan. This sweet and fluffy bread loaf is studded with candied fruits, raisins, and citrus zest, creating a delightful contrast of flavors and textures. Visitors can find authentic Panettone at bakeries and pastry shops throughout Milan, with prices varying depending on the size and quality of the cake. A small Panettone typically costs around €10 to €20, while larger sizes may range from €20 to €50 or more.

Ossobuco

Ossobuco, which translates to "bone with a hole," is a hearty Milanese stew made with braised veal shanks cooked in a flavorful broth of white wine, vegetables, and aromatic herbs. This comforting dish is often served with a gremolata—a zesty mixture of parsley, garlic, and lemon zest—sprinkled on top for added freshness and flavor. Visitors can enjoy Ossobuco at traditional Milanese trattorias and osterias, where it is typically priced between €20 to €40 per serving, depending on the size and presentation.

Tortelli di Zucca

Tortelli di Zucca, or pumpkin ravioli, is a traditional Lombard dish popular in Milan and the surrounding region. These delicate pasta parcels are filled with a creamy mixture of roasted pumpkin, Parmesan cheese, and nutmeg, then dressed in a butter and sage sauce for a comforting and savory flavor profile. Visitors can sample Tortelli di Zucca at local pasta shops and restaurants specializing in regional cuisine, with prices typically ranging from €15 to €25 per serving.

Cassoeula

Cassoeula is a rustic Milanese stew made with pork ribs, sausages, and cabbage, simmered together to create a rich and hearty dish that's perfect for chilly winter evenings. This traditional comfort food is often enjoyed during the colder months, with its robust flavors and tender meat making it a favorite among locals and visitors alike. Visitors can find Cassoeula on the menus of traditional Milanese trattorias and osterias, with prices ranging from €15 to €30 per serving, depending on the restaurant and portion size

Exploring the traditional Milanese cuisine offers visitors a delightful culinary journey through centuries-old recipes, local ingredients, and regional specialties that reflect the city's cultural heritage and gastronomic prowess. From iconic dishes like Risotto alla Milanese and Cotoletta alla Milanese to indulgent desserts like Panettone, Milanese cuisine showcases the diversity and richness of Lombard culinary traditions. By sampling these traditional dishes at local trattorias and restaurants, visitors can savor the authentic flavors of Milan and immerse themselves in the city's vibrant food culture.

6.2 Fine Dining Experiences

Milan, known as Italy's fashion and design capital, also boasts a Milan boasts a vibrant culinary scene that mirrors the city's rich cultural heritage and cosmopolitan influences. From traditional trattorias serving up authentic Milanese cuisine to Michelin-starred restaurants pushing the boundaries of gastronomy, Milan offers a diverse array of fine dining experiences for visitors to savor and enjoy. In this guide, we'll explore exceptional dining establishments where visitors can indulge in exquisite cuisine and unparalleled culinary craftsmanship.

Ristorante Trussardi alla Scala

Nestled in the heart of Milan's historic center, Ristorante Trussardi alla Scala offers a refined dining experience within the elegant setting of the Trussardi alla Scala boutique hotel. Helmed by acclaimed chef Luigi Taglienti, the restaurant showcases innovative interpretations of Italian classics using the finest seasonal ingredients. Diners can expect dishes such as risotto with saffron and gold leaf, veal Milanese with potato puree, and decadent desserts like tiramisu with a modern twist. Prices range from €80 to €150 per person for a multi-course tasting menu, excluding beverages.

Il Luogo di Aimo e Nadia

Il Luogo di Aimo e Nadia is a culinary institution in Milan, renowned for its creative approach to traditional Tuscan cuisine. Located in the quiet outskirts of the city, this Michelin-starred restaurant offers an intimate dining experience in a stylishly minimalist setting. Chef Stefania Moroni delights diners with seasonal tasting menus featuring dishes such as handmade pasta with wild boar ragu, slow-roasted Chianina beef with aromatic herbs, and delicate desserts infused with Tuscan flavors. Prices start from €120 per person for a tasting menu, excluding wine pairings.

Cracco

Situated in the heart of Milan's fashion district, Cracco is the eponymous restaurant of chef Carlo Cracco, a culinary visionary known for his innovative approach to Italian cuisine. Housed within a historic 19th-century palazzo, the restaurant offers a luxurious dining experience with sleek, contemporary decor and panoramic views of Milan's skyline. Guests can indulge in a gastronomic journey through Cracco's inventive dishes, such as spaghetti with sea urchin and lemon zest, slow-cooked veal cheek with black truffle, and imaginative desserts like chocolate spheres filled with liquid nitrogen. Prices range from €150 to €250 per person for a tasting menu, excluding beverages.

Joia

For visitors seeking a plant-based dining experience, Joia offers a Michelin-starred culinary journey showcasing the artistry of vegetarian and vegan cuisine. Located in the vibrant Porta Nuova district, the restaurant celebrates seasonal produce and sustainable ingredients in its creative dishes. Chef Pietro Leemann's menu features inventive creations such as beetroot tartare with avocado mousse, saffron risotto with seasonal vegetables, and indulgent vegan desserts like chocolate fondant with raspberry coulis. Prices start from €80 per person for a tasting menu, excluding beverages.

Il Luogo di Aimo e Nadia

Il Luogo di Aimo e Nadia is a culinary institution in Milan, renowned for its creative approach to traditional Tuscan cuisine. Located in the quiet outskirts of the city, this Michelin-starred restaurant offers an intimate dining experience in a stylishly minimalist setting. Chef Stefania Moroni delights diners with seasonal tasting menus featuring dishes such as handmade pasta with wild boar ragu, slow-roasted Chianina beef with aromatic herbs, and delicate desserts infused with Tuscan flavors. Prices start from €120 per person for a tasting menu, excluding wine pairings.

Sadler

Sadler is the brainchild of chef Claudio Sadler, a celebrated figure in Milan's culinary scene known for his mastery of modern Italian cuisine. Located in the charming district of Porta Romana, the restaurant exudes sophistication with its sleek, contemporary decor and impeccable service. Chef Sadler's menu showcases inventive dishes that marry traditional flavors with innovative techniques, such as foie gras ravioli with black truffle, roasted sea bass with fennel puree, and artfully plated desserts like white chocolate mousse with passion fruit sorbet. Prices range from €150 to €200 per person for a tasting menu, excluding beverages. Milan's fine dining scene offers a tantalizing array of culinary experiences for visitors to savor and enjoy. From Michelin-starred restaurants pushing the boundaries of gastronomy to intimate trattorias serving up authentic Italian flavors, there's something to suit every palate and occasion in this dynamic city. Whether indulging in innovative tasting menus or savoring traditional regional specialties, dining in Milan is sure to be a memorable and gastronomic journey for food enthusiasts from around the world.

6.3 Street Food and Markets

One of the most exciting ways to experience the vibrant food culture of Milan is by exploring its diverse street food offerings and bustling markets. From savory snacks served on-the-go to fresh produce and artisanal delicacies, Milan's streets and markets are teeming with culinary delights waiting to be discovered. In this guide, we'll delve into six must-visit street food vendors and markets in Milan, offering visitors a taste of the city's gastronomic treasures.

Panzerotti Luini

Tucked away in the heart of Milan's historic center, Panzerotti Luini is a beloved institution known for its iconic fried pastries filled with an array of delicious fillings. Established in 1888, this family-owned bakery continues to attract locals and tourists alike with its mouthwatering panzerotti, a type of savory turnover. Visitors can choose from classic fillings such as mozzarella and tomato, or indulge in gourmet options like prosciutto and gorgonzola. Prices range from €3 to €5 per panzerotto, making it an affordable and satisfying snack for exploring the city.

Mercato Metropolitano

Mercato Metropolitano is a sprawling food market located in Milan's Navigli district, offering a vibrant mix of street food stalls, artisanal producers, and communal dining spaces. Spanning over 15,000 square meters, this indoor-outdoor market is a food lover's paradise, showcasing a diverse range of cuisines from around the world. Visitors can sample freshly prepared dishes such as Neapolitan pizza, Sicilian arancini, and Tuscan porchetta, or browse the market's stalls for organic produce, cheese, and gourmet products. Prices vary depending on the vendor and dish, with most street food items ranging from €5 to €10.

Pizzeria Da Baffetto

For an authentic taste of Naples in Milan, look no further than Pizzeria Da Baffetto, a charming pizzeria located near the Porta Genova train station. This family-run eatery has been serving up traditional Neapolitan pizza since 1961, earning a loyal following for its thin, crispy crusts and flavorful toppings. Visitors can enjoy classic pizzas such as margherita, marinara, and capricciosa, cooked to perfection in a wood-fired oven. Prices for a pizza range from €8 to €12, making it an affordable and satisfying option for a quick meal.

Mercato di Via Papiniano

Mercato di Via Papiniano is one of Milan's oldest and most vibrant open-air markets, offering a wide selection of fresh produce, meats, seafood, and specialty foods. Located in the lively Porta Ticinese neighborhood, this bustling market is a favorite among locals for its lively atmosphere and diverse offerings. Visitors can wander through the market's stalls, sampling seasonal fruits and vegetables, selecting cuts of meat for a barbecue, or indulging in freshly baked bread and pastries. Prices at the market vary depending on the vendor and product, with plenty of affordable options for budget-conscious travelers.

Food Truck Festival Milan

For a taste of street food from around the world, visitors should check out the Food Truck Festival Milan, a recurring event held in various locations throughout the city. This popular food festival brings together a diverse lineup of food trucks and vendors, offering an eclectic array of culinary delights to sample and enjoy. From gourmet burgers and tacos to artisanal ice cream and craft beer, there's something to satisfy every craving at this dynamic event. Prices for food truck offerings typically range from €5 to €15 per item, making it an affordable and fun way to experience Milan's street food scene.

Gelateria Grom

No visit to Milan would be complete without indulging in Italy's iconic gelato, and Gelateria Grom is the perfect place to satisfy your sweet tooth. With multiple locations throughout the city, including near the Duomo and Navigli canals, Gelateria Grom is renowned for its high-quality, all-natural gelato made from fresh, seasonal ingredients. Visitors can choose from a variety of classic and innovative flavors, such as pistachio, stracciatella, and hazelnut, all served in freshly made waffle cones or cups. Prices for a gelato cone start from €3, making it a delicious and affordable treat for exploring Milan's sights and attractions. Exploring Milan's street food vendors and markets is an exciting way to immerse yourself in the city's culinary culture and sample a diverse range of flavors and specialties. From savory panzerotti and traditional Neapolitan pizza to fresh produce and artisanal gelato, there's something to delight every palate in Milan's bustling streets and markets. Whether you're strolling through the Mercato Metropolitano or indulging in a sweet treat at Gelateria Grom, each culinary experience offers a unique glimpse into the vibrant food scene of this cosmopolitan city.

6.4 Wine Bars and Aperitivo Culture

Milan's vibrant wine bars and aperitivo culture offer visitors a unique opportunity to experience the city's convivial atmosphere and culinary delights. Aperitivo, the Italian tradition of enjoying pre-dinner drinks accompanied by appetizers, has become a beloved ritual in Milan, with locals and tourists alike gathering in wine bars and cafes to unwind and socialize after a day of exploration. In this guide, we'll explore six exceptional wine bars where visitors can savor fine wines, indulge in delectable appetizers, and immerse themselves in Milan's lively aperitivo culture.

Cantine Isola

Located in the charming Isola district, Cantine Isola is a cozy wine bar and enoteca known for its extensive selection of Italian wines and artisanal cheeses. The bar's rustic yet inviting ambiance makes it a popular spot for locals and visitors seeking an authentic aperitivo experience. Guests can choose from a wide range of wines by the glass or bottle, accompanied by a curated selection of cheese and charcuterie boards. Prices for wine by the glass start from €5, with cheese and charcuterie boards ranging from €10 to €20.

N'ombra de Vin

Tucked away in a picturesque alley near the Brera district, N'ombra de Vin is a hidden gem renowned for its intimate atmosphere and impressive wine list. The bar offers an extensive selection of Italian and international wines, as well as a variety of small plates and appetizers to complement the wine tasting experience. Visitors can relax on the outdoor terrace or cozy up indoors while enjoying a glass of wine paired with gourmet snacks such as bruschetta, olives, and crostini. Prices for wine by the glass range from €6 to €12, with appetizers starting at €8.

Radetzky Café

Situated in Milan's trendy Porta Venezia neighborhood, Radetzky Café is a stylish yet laid-back wine bar and cafe popular among locals and expats. The bar's chic decor and outdoor seating make it the perfect spot for people-watching while enjoying an aperitivo. Guests can choose from an extensive wine list featuring Italian and international varietals, as well as classic cocktails and spritzes. Complement your drink with a selection of light bites and snacks, including gourmet sandwiches, salads, and antipasti platters. Prices for drinks start from €5, with appetizers ranging from €8 to €15.

Cinc

Cinc is a contemporary wine bar located in Milan's vibrant Navigli district, known for its lively nightlife and picturesque canal views. The bar's sleek interior and industrial-chic decor create a trendy yet relaxed atmosphere, perfect for enjoying an evening aperitivo with friends. Guests can choose from an extensive wine list featuring Italian and international labels, as well as craft cocktails and spirits. Pair your drink with a selection of small plates and sharing dishes, including bruschetta, cheese boards, and seafood crudo. Prices for drinks start from €6, with appetizers ranging from €10 to €18.

Deus Café

Deus Café is a hip and eclectic wine bar located in the vibrant Porta Genova district, known for its bohemian vibe and artistic flair. The bar's quirky decor and laid-back ambiance make it a popular hangout for Milan's creative crowd, offering a unique setting for enjoying an aperitivo. Guests can choose from a diverse selection of wines, beers, and cocktails, as well as a variety of vegetarian and vegan-friendly snacks and small plates. Prices for drinks start from €5, with appetizers ranging from €8 to €15.

Rinomata Aperitivi

Rinomata Aperitivi is a charming wine bar and aperitivo spot located in the Located in the heart of Milan's historic center, mere steps away from the iconic Duomo cathedral. The bar's elegant decor and cozy atmosphere make it a favorite among locals and tourists alike, offering a refined setting for enjoying an evening drink. Guests can choose from an extensive wine list featuring Italian classics and international favorites, as well as signature cocktails and spritzes. Pair your drink with a selection of gourmet appetizers, including bruschetta, artisanal cheeses, and cured meats. Prices for drinks start from €7, with appetizers ranging from €10 to €20. Milan's wine bars and aperitivo culture offer visitors a delightful opportunity to unwind and socialize while savoring the flavors of Italy. Whether you're sipping wine in a cozy enoteca or enjoying cocktails on a trendy terrace, each wine bar offers a unique ambiance and selection of drinks and appetizers to suit every taste and occasion. Embrace the spirit of Italian hospitality and join locals in the time-honored tradition of aperitivo, as you soak up the vibrant atmosphere and culinary delights of Milan's bustling streets and neighborhoods.

6.5 Cooking Classes and Food Tours

Milan, renowned for its fashion, design, and culture, is also a paradise for food enthusiasts eager to explore the rich gastronomic traditions of Italy. For visitors looking to immerse themselves in Milan's culinary scene, cooking classes and food tours offer hands-on experiences and insider insights into the city's vibrant food culture. In this guide, we'll delve into six exceptional cooking classes and food tours where visitors can learn to prepare authentic Italian dishes, sample local specialties, and discover the flavors of Milan.

Pasta Making Class at La Cucina Italiana: La Cucina Italiana, a renowned culinary magazine, offers pasta making classes in Milan for those eager to learn the art of creating fresh pasta from scratch. Led by experienced chefs, these hands-on classes take place in a professional kitchen setting and cover techniques for making various types of pasta, including tagliatelle, ravioli, and gnocchi. Participants learn to knead dough, roll out pasta sheets, and shape pasta by hand, before enjoying their creations paired with classic Italian sauces. Prices for pasta making classes at La Cucina Italiana start from €70 per person, and advance booking is recommended.

Food Tour of Milan with Walks of Italy
Walks of Italy offers guided food tours of Milan, providing visitors with a culinary journey through the city's diverse neighborhoods and markets. Led by knowledgeable local guides, these walking tours introduce participants to Milan's culinary traditions, artisanal producers, and hidden gems. Highlights of the tour may include visits to traditional bakeries, cheese shops, and gelaterias, as well as tastings of regional specialties such as panettone, risotto, and Milanese salami. Prices for food tours with Walks of Italy start from €80 per person, and reservations are required.

Pizza Making Workshop at Rossopomodoro
Rossopomodoro, a popular pizzeria chain in Italy, offers pizza making workshops in Milan for visitors keen to learn the secrets of crafting authentic Neapolitan pizza. Led by expert pizzaiolos, these interactive workshops teach participants the techniques for making pizza dough, stretching it by hand, and topping it with fresh ingredients. Participants have the opportunity to customize their pizzas with a variety of toppings, before watching them bake in a wood-fired oven. Prices for pizza making workshops at Rossopomodoro start from €40 per person, and advance booking is recommended.

Market Tour and Cooking Class at Eataly Milano Smeraldo
Eataly Milano Smeraldo, a renowned food market and culinary destination, offers market tours and cooking classes for visitors interested in Italian cuisine. Led by professional chefs, these immersive experiences begin with a guided tour of Eataly's market stalls, where participants learn about the quality and provenance of ingredients used in Italian cooking. Following the tour, participants return to the kitchen to prepare a

multi-course meal using seasonal produce and artisanal products sourced from the market. Prices for market tours and cooking classes at Eataly Milano Smeraldo start from €90 per person, and reservations are recommended.

Gelato Making Workshop at Gelato Giusto

Gelato Giusto, a renowned gelateria in Milan, offers gelato making workshops for visitors eager to learn the art of crafting authentic Italian gelato. Led by skilled gelato makers, these hands-on workshops take participants behind the scenes of the gelateria to learn about the ingredients and techniques used in gelato production. Participants have the opportunity to mix and churn their own gelato flavors, experimenting with a variety of ingredients and flavors. Prices for gelato making workshops at Gelato Giusto start from €50 per person, and advance booking is required.

Wine Tasting Experience at Vinodromo

Vinodromo, a boutique wine shop and tasting room in Milan, offers wine tasting experiences for visitors keen to explore Italy's rich viticultural heritage. Led by knowledgeable sommeliers, these guided tastings introduce participants to a selection of Italian wines, including regional varietals and lesser-known gems. Participants learn about wine production methods, tasting techniques, and food pairing suggestions while sampling a curated selection of wines accompanied by artisanal snacks. Prices for wine tasting experiences at Vinodromo start from €30 per person, and reservations are recommended.

Cooking classes and food tours offer visitors a unique opportunity to immerse themselves in Milan's culinary culture and discover the flavors of Italy. Whether learning to make fresh pasta, exploring local markets, or tasting regional wines, each experience provides valuable insights into the traditions and techniques that define Italian cuisine. By participating in these hands-on experiences, visitors can gain a deeper appreciation for Milan's gastronomic heritage and create lasting memories of their time in the city.

CHAPTER 7
CULTURE AND HERITAGE

7.1 Historical Landmarks and Monuments

Milan, the fashion capital of Italy, boasts not only trendy boutiques and exquisite cuisine but also a rich tapestry of history and culture, reflected in its remarkable landmarks and monuments. From grand cathedrals to historic fortresses, Milan's architectural marvels invite visitors to immerse themselves in the city's captivating past. Let's delve into six of Milan's most prominent historical landmarks and monuments, each offering a unique glimpse into the city's heritage.

Milan Cathedral (Duomo di Milano)
Standing proudly at the heart of Milan, the Milan Cathedral, or Duomo di Milano, is an awe-inspiring masterpiece of Gothic architecture. Its magnificent façade, adorned with intricate sculptures and spires, mesmerizes visitors from afar. Located in Piazza del Duomo, the cathedral is easily accessible by public transportation, with nearby metro and tram stations.

Entrance to the cathedral is free, but if you wish to explore its interior, including the archaeological area and the rooftop terraces, tickets are available for a nominal fee. The climb to the rooftop offers panoramic views of Milan's skyline, making it a must-do for visitors seeking a unique perspective of the city. Beyond its architectural splendor, the

Milan Cathedral holds significant historical and cultural importance. Construction began in the 14th century and continued for centuries, symbolizing the city's enduring faith and resilience. Inside, visitors can admire exquisite stained glass windows, intricate marble carvings, and the impressive central nave.

Sforza Castle (Castello Sforzesco)

Embracing Milan's skyline with its imposing presence, the Sforza Castle stands as a testament to the city's medieval heritage. Originally built in the 15th century by the powerful Sforza dynasty, the castle served as a symbol of their dominance and later underwent extensive renovations under various rulers. Located in Parco Sempione, the castle is easily reachable by public transport, including metro and bus services. Entry to the castle is free, allowing visitors to explore its expansive grounds, lush courtyards, and museums.

The Sforza Castle houses several museums, including the Museum of Ancient Art, showcasing works by renowned artists such as Michelangelo and da Vinci. Visitors can also admire Michelangelo's unfinished masterpiece, the Pietà Rondanini, housed within the castle walls.

Santa Maria delle Grazie

Nestled within the bustling streets of Milan lies the Santa Maria delle Grazie, a UNESCO World Heritage Site renowned for housing one of the world's most famous artworks – Leonardo da Vinci's "The Last Supper." This 15th-century church, adorned with Renaissance architecture, beckons visitors to witness its cultural treasures. Located in the heart of Milan, near the Cadorna metro station, Santa Maria delle Grazie is easily accessible for visitors. While entry to the church is free, reservations are essential to view "The Last Supper" due to its popularity and limited viewing slots.

"The Last Supper" is an iconic masterpiece depicting the biblical scene of Jesus dining with his disciples. Visitors can marvel at da Vinci's meticulous brushwork and the emotional depth conveyed in this renowned fresco. Beyond the artwork, the church's serene ambiance and architectural beauty offer a tranquil retreat from the city's hustle and bustle.

Galleria Vittorio Emanuele II

Draped in elegance and opulence, the Galleria Vittorio Emanuele II stands as a testament to Milan's status as a global fashion capital. This 19th-century shopping arcade, named after Italy's first king, boasts stunning architecture and a wealth of luxury boutiques, cafes, and restaurants. Located adjacent to the Milan Cathedral in Piazza del Duomo, the Galleria is easily accessible on foot or by public transport. Entry to the arcade is free, welcoming visitors to stroll through its marble corridors and admire its ornate glass dome. While the Galleria is renowned for its high-end shopping, it also holds historical significance as one of the world's oldest shopping malls. Visitors can marvel at its intricate mosaics, elegant storefronts, and the iconic bull mosaic on the floor, believed to bring good luck when spun three times.

San Maurizio al Monastero Maggiore

Tucked away from the bustling streets of Milan, San Maurizio al Monastero Maggiore offers a hidden gem for art and history enthusiasts. This 16th-century church, often referred to as the "Sistine Chapel of Milan," boasts breathtaking frescoes and ornate decorations that rival those of its more famous counterpart. Located near the Porta Venezia metro station, San Maurizio al Monastero Maggiore is easily accessible for visitors. Entry to the church is free, allowing visitors to immerse themselves in its serene atmosphere and admire its artistic treasures.

The church's interior is adorned with exquisite frescoes depicting biblical scenes, intricate details, and vibrant colors that captivate the imagination. Visitors can wander through its aisles, marveling at the craftsmanship of artists such as Bernardino Luini and Giovanni Battista della Rovere.

Brera Art Gallery (Pinacoteca di Brera)

Nestled in the historic Brera district, the Brera Art Gallery stands as a cultural oasis, housing an impressive collection of Italian artworks spanning centuries. Founded in the late 18th century, this prestigious gallery showcases masterpieces by renowned artists such as Raphael, Caravaggio, and Titian. Located near the Moscova metro station, the Brera Art Gallery is easily accessible for visitors. While entry fees apply, the gallery offers discounted rates for students and free admission on certain days of the week, making it accessible to a wide audience. Inside the gallery, visitors can explore a diverse range of artistic styles, from Renaissance classics to Baroque treasures. Highlights include Raphael's "The Marriage of the Virgin," Caravaggio's "Supper at Emmaus," and Bellini's "Pieta." The gallery's tranquil ambiance and curated exhibitions offer an enriching experience for art aficionados and casual visitors alike.

Milan's historical landmarks and monuments offer a captivating journey through the city's rich heritage and cultural legacy. From the awe-inspiring Milan Cathedral to the hidden gems of San Maurizio al Monastero Maggiore, each site invites visitors to explore centuries of history, art, and architecture. Whether you're drawn to iconic masterpieces, medieval fortresses, or Renaissance splendor, Milan's treasures promise an unforgettable experience for every discerning traveler. So, pack your bags, embark on a journey through time, and discover the timeless charm of Milan's historical gems.

7.2 Art and Architecture

Milan, the vibrant cultural capital of Italy, is renowned for its rich artistic heritage and breathtaking architecture. From majestic palaces to world-class museums, the city's artistic treasures offer a feast for the senses. Let's delve into six remarkable examples of Milan's arts and architecture, each showcasing the city's creative spirit and historical significance.

La Scala Opera House

Nestled in the heart of Milan, La Scala Opera House, or Teatro alla Scala, stands as a beacon of classical music and performing arts. Dating back to the 18th century, this iconic theater has hosted some of the world's most celebrated opera performances, ballets, and concerts, earning its place as one of the most prestigious venues in the world. Located in Piazza della Scala, La Scala is easily accessible by public transportation, including metro and tram services. While tickets for performances may vary in price, visitors can also explore the theater's museum Visitors can also participate in guided tours to marvel at the church's lavish interiors and gain insights into its remarkable history. Beyond its architectural grandeur, La Scala holds immense cultural significance, having nurtured and showcased the talents of countless opera legends over the centuries. Visitors can immerse themselves in the rich ambiance of this historic venue, attending a live performance or simply marveling at its elegant façade and exquisite interior décor.

Leonardo da Vinci National Museum of Science and Technology
Dedicated to one of history's greatest minds, the Leonardo da Vinci National Museum of Science and Technology offers a fascinating journey through the realms of art, science, and innovation. Housed within a former monastery in the heart of Milan, this museum boasts an extensive collection of exhibits, interactive displays, and Leonardo's groundbreaking inventions. Located in Via San Vittore, the museum is easily reachable by public transport, with nearby metro and bus stops. Entry fees may apply, with discounts available for students and children, making it an accessible destination for all ages. Visitors to the museum can explore Leonardo's inventions, from flying machines to anatomical studies, gaining insight into his revolutionary ideas and visionary genius. Interactive workshops and educational programs offer hands-on experiences for curious minds, making it an ideal destination for families and enthusiasts alike.

Triennale di Milano
Embracing the spirit of innovation and contemporary design, the Triennale di Milano stands as a cultural hub for art, architecture, and design enthusiasts. Located within the historic Palazzo dell'Arte in Parco Sempione, this institution hosts exhibitions, installations, and events that showcase cutting-edge creativity from around the world. Accessible via public transportation, including metro and tram services, the Triennale di

Milano welcomes visitors with its striking modernist architecture and lush surroundings. Entry fees may vary depending on exhibitions and events, with discounts available for students and seniors. Visitors can immerse themselves in a diverse array of artistic expressions, from avant-garde installations to thought-provoking design showcases. The museum's rotating exhibitions and thematic programs offer fresh perspectives on contemporary culture and creativity, making it a dynamic destination for cultural exploration.

Bosco Verticale (Vertical Forest)

Reimagining urban living and sustainability, the Bosco Verticale, or Vertical Forest, stands as a testament to innovative architecture and ecological design. Situated within the dynamic Porta Nuova district, these residential towers are embellished with lush greenery, creating a vertical forest that purifies the air and enhances the cityscape. Accessible via public transport, the Bosco Verticale offers guided tours for visitors interested in exploring its eco-friendly features and sustainable design principles. While entry to the towers may be restricted to residents, the surrounding area provides ample opportunities to admire its striking façade and lush vegetation.

Visitors can marvel at the juxtaposition of nature and architecture, as the towers' verdant balconies create a stunning visual spectacle against Milan's skyline. The Bosco Verticale serves as a pioneering example of sustainable urban development, inspiring cities around the world to embrace green design solutions for a healthier, more livable future.

Palazzo Reale

Embracing Milan's regal past and artistic legacy, the Palazzo Reale, or Royal Palace, stands as a majestic symbol of power and elegance. Dating back to the Middle Ages, this historic palace has served as a residence for noble families and rulers, bearing witness to centuries of political intrigue and cultural patronage. Located in Piazza del Duomo, the Palazzo Reale is easily accessible on foot or by public transportation, with nearby metro and tram stations. Entry fees may apply for special exhibitions and guided tours, allowing visitors to explore its lavish interiors and admire its priceless art collections.

Visitors can wander through opulent salons, grand ballrooms, and royal chambers adorned with masterpieces by renowned artists such as Tiepolo, Canaletto, and Hayez. The palace's rich history and architectural splendor offer a glimpse into Milan's royal past, transporting visitors to a bygone era of aristocratic grandeur and cultural refinement.

Fondazione Prada

Fusing contemporary art with architectural innovation, the Fondazione Prada stands as a beacon of creativity and cultural experimentation. Designed by renowned architect Rem Koolhaas, this sprawling complex in Largo Isarco showcases cutting-edge exhibitions, installations, and performances that push the boundaries of artistic expression. Accessible via public transportation, including metro and bus services, the Fondazione Prada welcomes visitors with its striking industrial-chic architecture and vibrant cultural programming. Entry fees may apply for exhibitions and events, with discounts available for students and art enthusiasts.

Visitors can explore a diverse range of contemporary artworks, from multimedia installations to avant-garde performances, curated by leading artists and curators from around the world. The foundation's dynamic events and interdisciplinary approach offer a stimulating environment for dialogue and exploration, rendering it an essential destination for aficionados of art and cultural enthusiasts alike.

Milan's arts and architecture embody the city's rich heritage, creative vitality, and cosmopolitan spirit. From the grandeur of La Scala Opera House to the innovation of the Bosco Verticale, each landmark and institution offers a unique window into Milan's cultural landscape, inviting visitors to explore, engage, and be inspired. So, whether you're drawn to classical masterpieces or contemporary design, embark on a journey through Milan's artistic treasures and discover the timeless allure of this dynamic metropolis.

7.3 Performing Arts and Cultural Events

Milan offers a vibrant array of performing arts and cultural events that captivate locals and visitors alike. From world-class opera performances to dynamic theater productions, the city's cultural calendar brims with excitement year-round. Let's delve into six captivating examples of Milan's performing arts and cultural events, each offering a unique window into the city's artistic soul.

La Scala Opera Season

At the heart of Milan's cultural scene lies La Scala Opera House, renowned worldwide for its legendary opera productions. Located in Piazza della Scala, this historic theater has been hosting opera performances since the 18th century, showcasing the talents of opera's greatest luminaries. Accessible via public transportation, including metro and tram services, La Scala beckons visitors with its majestic façade and regal interiors. Tickets for opera performances vary in price, with options ranging from premium seats to standing room tickets for budget-conscious enthusiasts.

Attending a performance at La Scala is an unforgettable experience, steeped in tradition and artistry. From classic operas by Verdi and Puccini to contemporary works by modern composers, each production dazzles with world-class singing, lavish sets, and stirring orchestral music. Whether you're an opera aficionado or a first-time attendee, La Scala's opera season promises an immersive journey into the realm of music and drama.

Milan Fashion Week

Twice a year, Milan transforms into a global fashion capital during Milan Fashion Week, a glamorous extravaganza showcasing the latest trends and haute couture creations from top designers. Held in various locations across the city, including the iconic Galleria

Vittorio Emanuele II and Palazzo Reale, Fashion Week attracts industry insiders, celebrities, and fashion enthusiasts from around the world.

Getting to Milan Fashion Week venues is convenient, with ample public transportation options and taxi services available throughout the city. While entry to official runway shows is by invitation only, fashion aficionados can soak up the atmosphere by attending public events, exhibitions, and parties hosted by fashion houses and luxury brands. Milan Fashion Week is not just a showcase of style but also a celebration of creativity, innovation, and cultural heritage. From glamorous runway presentations to avant-garde installations, the event offers a glimpse into the evolving landscape of fashion and design. Visitors can explore pop-up shops, attend panel discussions, and mingle with industry insiders, immersing themselves in Milan's dynamic fashion scene.

Piccolo Teatro di Milano
Founded in 1947 by renowned theater director Giorgio Strehler, the Piccolo Teatro di Milano is Italy's first permanent repertory theater, dedicated to promoting innovative and socially relevant theatrical productions. Located in the heart of Milan's historic district, this esteemed cultural institution presents a diverse repertoire of classic and contemporary plays, performed by talented actors and directors. Accessible by public transportation, the Piccolo Teatro di Milano is situated near several metro and tram stops, making it easily reachable for theatergoers. Ticket prices vary depending on the production and seating preferences, with discounts available for students and seniors.

Attending a performance at the Piccolo Teatro is a cultural immersion into the world of theater, where storytelling comes to life on stage. From timeless classics by Shakespeare and Chekhov to cutting-edge works by contemporary playwrights, each production captivates audiences with its thought-provoking themes, compelling performances, and innovative staging. Visitors can also participate in workshops, talks, and events organized by the theater, fostering dialogue and engagement with the arts.

Milan Film Festival

Every fall, Milan hosts the Milan Film Festival, a dynamic celebration of cinema that showcases a diverse selection of international and Italian films, documentaries, and short films. Held at various venues across the city, including cinemas, theaters, and cultural institutions, The festival draws filmmakers, industry experts, and cinema enthusiasts from various corners of the globe. Getting to Milan Film Festival screenings is convenient, with public transportation options available to reach different venues throughout the city. Ticket prices vary depending on the screening and event, with discounts often available for students and festival pass holders.

The Milan Film Festival offers a platform for emerging talent and established filmmakers to showcase their works, providing audiences with a rich tapestry of cinematic experiences. From avant-garde indie films to blockbuster premieres, the festival celebrates diversity, creativity, and storytelling in all its forms. Visitors can attend screenings, Q&A sessions with filmmakers, and special events, immersing themselves in the magic of cinema and engaging with the global film community.

Milano Musica Festival

For lovers of classical music and contemporary compositions, Milano Musica Festival offers a feast for the ears, presenting a diverse program of orchestral concerts, chamber music recitals, and avant-garde performances. Held at various venues across Milan, including concert halls, churches, and cultural centers, the festival showcases renowned musicians and emerging talents from around the world. Accessible via public transportation, Milano Musica Festival venues are conveniently located near metro and tram stops, making it easy for concertgoers to attend performances. Ticket prices vary depending on the concert and seating category, with discounts often available for students and subscribers.

Attending Milano Musica Festival concerts is an enriching experience, where audiences can savor the sublime beauty of classical masterpieces and explore the cutting-edge sounds of contemporary music. From orchestral symphonies to experimental electronic compositions, each performance captivates with its virtuosity, passion, and innovation. Visitors can also participate in pre-concert talks, workshops, and masterclasses, deepening their appreciation for music and connecting with fellow enthusiasts.

Milan Jazz Festival

For aficionados of jazz music, the Milan Jazz Festival offers a thrilling showcase of talent, featuring world-class performers, improvisers, and ensembles from the vibrant jazz scene. Held at various venues across the city, including concert halls, clubs, and outdoor stages, The festival showcases a varied array of jazz genres, spanning from classic swing to modern fusion. Navigating the Milan Jazz Festival venues is easy, with public transportation options available to reach different locations throughout the city. Ticket prices vary depending on the concert and seating arrangement, with discounts often available for students and jazz club members.

Attending Milan Jazz Festival concerts is a sensory delight, where audiences can groove to the infectious rhythms, intricate melodies, and spontaneous improvisations of jazz music. From intimate club gigs to large-scale outdoor performances, each concert offers a unique sonic experience, steeped in the rich traditions and innovative spirit of jazz. Visitors can also participate in jam sessions, workshops, and educational events, fostering community engagement and artistic exchange.

Milan's performing arts and cultural events offer a dynamic tapestry of experiences, enriching the city's cultural landscape and delighting audiences from near and far. Whether you're drawn to the grandeur of opera at La Scala, the avant-garde productions at Piccolo Teatro, or the pulsating rhythms of jazz at Milan Jazz Festival, the city's cultural calendar promises something for everyone. So, immerse yourself in the magic of Milan's performing arts scene, and let the city's creative spirit ignite your imagination and inspire your soul.

7.4 Religious Sites and Festivals

Milan, a city steeped in history and tradition, is home to an array of religious sites and festivals that reflect its rich spiritual heritage. From magnificent cathedrals to sacred celebrations, these sites and events offer visitors a profound glimpse into Milan's cultural and religious identity. Let's delve into six captivating examples of Milan's religious sites and festivals, each offering a unique spiritual experience.

Milan Cathedral (Duomo di Milano)

At the heart of Milan stands the awe-inspiring Milan Cathedral, or Duomo di Milano, a magnificent testament to faith and architectural splendor. Located in Piazza del Duomo, this Gothic masterpiece is easily accessible by public transportation, with nearby metro and tram stations. Entry to the cathedral is free, allowing visitors to marvel at its intricate façade adorned with spires, statues, and elaborate carvings. For a nominal fee, visitors can explore the cathedral's interior, including its impressive nave, stained glass windows, and crypt.

The Milan Cathedral holds profound historical and spiritual significance, serving as a symbol of the city's enduring faith and cultural legacy. Construction began in the 14th century, and its completion took centuries, embodying the collective devotion of generations of Milanese. Visitors can attend mass, admire religious relics, and climb to the rooftop for panoramic views of the city.

Santa Maria delle Grazie

Nestled within Milan's bustling streets lies the UNESCO-listed Santa Maria delle Grazie, a sacred sanctuary renowned for housing Leonardo da Vinci's masterpiece, "The Last Supper." Located near the Cadorna metro station, the church is easily accessible for visitors. While entry to the church is free, reservations are essential to view "The Last Supper" due to its popularity and limited viewing slots. Visitors can witness da Vinci's iconic fresco depicting the biblical scene of Jesus and his disciples, showcasing the artist's mastery of perspective and emotion.

Santa Maria delle Grazie holds profound cultural and spiritual significance, serving as a place of worship and pilgrimage for centuries. The church's serene ambiance, Renaissance architecture, and religious artworks invite contemplation and reflection. Visitors can attend mass, explore the church's chapels and cloisters, and learn about its rich history through guided tours and exhibitions.

Basilica of Sant'Ambrogio

Steeped in antiquity and reverence, the Basilica of Sant'Ambrogio stands as one of Milan's oldest and most significant religious sites. Located in the historic district of Sant'Ambrogio, the basilica is easily reachable by public transportation, with nearby tram and bus stops. Entry to the basilica is free, welcoming visitors to explore its Romanesque architecture, ancient mosaics, and sacred relics. The crypt houses the relics of Saint Ambrose, Milan's patron saint, attracting pilgrims and devotees seeking spiritual solace.

The Basilica of Sant'Ambrogio holds profound historical and spiritual significance, dating back to the 4th century when it was founded by Saint Ambrose himself. Over the centuries, the basilica has played a central role in Milanese religious life, serving as a place of worship, pilgrimage, and cultural heritage. Visitors can attend mass, participate in religious ceremonies, and explore the basilica's museum, which houses precious artifacts and artworks.

Feast of Saint Ambrose (Festa di Sant'Ambrogio)

Each year on December 7th, Milan celebrates the Feast of Saint Ambrose, or Festa di Sant'Ambrogio, with joyous festivities and religious rituals. The celebration honors the legacy of Milan's patron saint, Saint Ambrose, and marks the beginning of the city's holiday season.

The Feast of Saint Ambrose is celebrated throughout Milan, with special events, processions, and religious services held at the Basilica of Sant'Ambrogio and other churches across the city. Visitors can join locals in paying homage to the saint, attending mass, and enjoying traditional foods and drinks. The Feast of Saint Ambrose holds profound cultural and religious significance, symbolizing the unity and resilience of Milanese identity. It offers visitors a unique opportunity to immerse themselves in Milan's spiritual traditions, witness vibrant street parades, and partake in communal celebrations that bridge the past and present.

San Bernardino alle Ossa

Tucked away in the heart of Milan lies the intriguing San Bernardino alle Ossa, a petite church celebrated for its unsettling ossuary decorated with human bones and skulls. Positioned close to the Duomo, this distinctive religious spot is readily reachable for inquisitive visitors. Admission to San Bernardino alle Ossa is complimentary, encouraging exploration of its eerie yet fascinating interior, where human remains are intricately arranged and displayed as a solemn reminder of mortality. The church's Baroque architecture and haunting décor offer a sobering reflection on the transient nature of life.

San Bernardino alle Ossa holds historical significance as a place of worship and contemplation, dating back to the 13th century when it was built adjacent to the nearby hospital and cemetery. Over the centuries, the church's ossuary became a site of pilgrimage and devotion, attracting visitors seeking solace and spiritual reflection.

Milan Easter Festival

Each spring, Milan hosts the Milan Easter Festival, a jubilant celebration of the resurrection of Jesus Christ featuring religious services, processions, and cultural events. Held at various churches and venues across the city, the festival brings together believers and visitors from diverse backgrounds to commemorate this sacred occasion.

The Milan Easter Festival offers a rich program of activities, including liturgical services, choral performances, and artistic exhibitions that explore the themes of faith, renewal, and redemption. Visitors can witness solemn processions, attend mass, and participate in traditional rituals that evoke the solemnity and joy of Easter. The Milan Easter Festival holds deep spiritual and cultural significance, uniting communities in prayer, reflection, and fellowship. It offers visitors a chance to experience Milan's religious traditions firsthand, immerse themselves in sacred music and art, and embrace the spiritual essence of Easter.

Milan's religious sites and festivals offer visitors a profound journey through the city's spiritual heritage and cultural traditions. From the grandeur of the Milan Cathedral to the solemnity of San Bernardino alle Ossa, each site invites contemplation, reflection, and reverence. Whether attending religious services, participating in sacred rituals, or joining festive celebrations, visitors can immerse themselves in Milan's rich tapestry of faith, history, and culture, finding solace and inspiration amidst the city's timeless landmarks and sacred traditions.

7.5 Preservation of Cultural Heritage in Milan

Milan, a city steeped in historical and cultural significance, is committed to safeguarding its cultural legacy through a range of initiatives and approaches. From architectural conservation to cultural institutions, Milan employs a multifaceted approach to safeguard its past for future generations. These are ways in which Milan preserves its cultural heritage, each offering a unique insight into the city's historical significance and cultural identity.

Architectural Conservation

One of the most visible ways Milan preserves its cultural heritage is through architectural conservation. The city is home to numerous historic buildings, palaces, and monuments dating back centuries, each with its own unique architectural style and significance. Through careful restoration and maintenance efforts, Milan ensures that these architectural treasures remain intact for generations to come.

Visitors to Milan can witness the city's architectural heritage firsthand by exploring iconic landmarks such as the Milan Cathedral, Sforza Castle, and Galleria Vittorio Emanuele II. These structures not only serve as symbols of Milan's illustrious past but also as living testaments to the city's commitment to preserving its cultural legacy. Tourists can admire the intricate details of Gothic cathedrals, stroll through Renaissance palaces, and marvel at the grandeur of Baroque churches, all while gaining a deeper appreciation for Milan's architectural heritage.

Museums and Cultural Institutions
Milan boasts a wealth of museums and cultural institutions dedicated to preserving and showcasing its artistic and historical heritage. From world-class art galleries to immersive history museums, these institutions offer visitors a comprehensive glimpse into Milan's cultural identity and evolution over time.

Visitors can explore renowned institutions such as the Pinacoteca di Brera, which houses an impressive collection of Italian masterpieces, or the Leonardo da Vinci National Museum of Science and Technology, which celebrates the genius of one of history's greatest minds. Additionally, Milan is home to cultural hubs like the Triennale di Milano, where contemporary design and innovation are celebrated through exhibitions and events. By patronizing these museums and cultural institutions, visitors not only gain insight into Milan's cultural heritage but also contribute to its preservation and continued relevance in the modern world. Through educational programs, temporary exhibitions, and outreach initiatives, these institutions play a vital role in fostering appreciation for Milan's rich artistic and historical legacy.

Preservation of Historic Districts
In addition to individual landmarks and buildings, Milan is committed to preserving its historic districts and neighborhoods, which serve as living embodiments of the city's cultural heritage. From the charming streets of Brera to the bustling Navigli canals, these districts offer visitors a glimpse into Milan's past while also serving as vibrant hubs of contemporary life.

Strolling through the cobblestone streets of Brera or along the picturesque canals of Navigli, visitors can admire the well-preserved architecture, quaint cafes, and artisanal shops that characterize these historic neighborhoods. These districts are not only popular destinations for tourists but also cherished spaces for locals, who take pride in their cultural heritage and work to maintain the authenticity and charm of these areas. Through zoning regulations, preservation initiatives, and community involvement, Milan ensures that its historic districts retain their unique character and sense of place. Visitors to these neighborhoods can immerse themselves in the city's history, culture, and everyday life, forging connections with the past while experiencing the vibrancy of contemporary Milan.

Cultural Events and Festivals
Milan's cultural calendar is filled with events and festivals that celebrate its rich heritage and traditions. From religious festivities to arts and music celebrations, these events offer visitors an opportunity to experience Milan's cultural diversity and creativity firsthand.

Throughout the year, Milan hosts a variety of cultural events, including the Milan Fashion Week, Milano Musica Festival, and Milan Jazz Festival, which showcase the city's contributions to fashion, music, and the arts. Additionally, religious festivals such as the Feast of Saint Ambrose and Easter celebrations offer insight into Milan's spiritual traditions and cultural customs. Attending these cultural events and festivals allows visitors to engage with Milan's cultural heritage in a dynamic and immersive way. Whether participating in street parades, attending performances, or sampling traditional cuisine, visitors can connect with the city's cultural identity and create lasting memories.

Preservation of Intangible Heritage
In addition to physical landmarks and artifacts, Milan places importance on preserving its intangible cultural heritage, including traditions, rituals, and oral histories passed down through generations. These intangible elements contribute to the fabric of Milan's cultural identity and play a crucial role in shaping its social cohesion and sense of community. Visitors to Milan can experience the city's intangible heritage through various activities, such as attending folk music performances, participating in traditional

craft workshops, or sampling regional cuisine at local markets. These experiences offer insight into Milan's cultural traditions and provide opportunities for cultural exchange and dialogue. Milan's commitment to preserving its intangible heritage ensures that these cultural practices and traditions continue to thrive in the modern world. By safeguarding traditional knowledge and promoting cultural diversity, Milan enriches its cultural landscape and fosters a sense of pride and belonging among its residents and visitors alike.

Community Engagement and Education

Finally, Milan actively engages its community in the preservation of its cultural heritage through educational programs, volunteer initiatives, and public outreach efforts. By fostering a sense of ownership and stewardship among residents, Milan ensures that its cultural heritage remains a shared responsibility and source of pride for all. Through guided tours, lectures, and workshops, visitors to Milan can learn about the city's cultural heritage from knowledgeable guides and experts. Additionally, volunteer opportunities allow individuals to contribute directly to preservation efforts, whether through conservation projects, archival work, or community events.

By involving the community in cultural heritage preservation, Milan fosters a sense of connection and belonging among its residents while also promoting awareness and appreciation of its rich history and traditions. Visitors to Milan can engage with locals, learn from their insights, and actively participate in preserving the city's cultural legacy for future generations.

Milan's dedication to preserving its cultural heritage is evident in its diverse array of initiatives and methods, from architectural conservation to community engagement. By safeguarding its landmarks, institutions, traditions, and intangible heritage, Milan ensures that its cultural legacy remains vibrant and relevant in the modern world. Visitors to Milan can immerse themselves in the city's rich history, culture, and traditions, forging connections with the past while experiencing the dynamic energy of contemporary Milan. Whether exploring historic landmarks, attending cultural events, or engaging with local communities, visitors can contribute to the ongoing preservation and celebration of Milan's cultural heritage, leaving a lasting impact on this iconic city.

CHAPTER 8
OUTDOOR ACTIVITIES AND ADVENTURES

8.1 City Parks and Urban Green Spaces

Milan is not only renowned for its historic landmarks and cultural attractions but also for its abundant green spaces and city parks.These urban retreats provide a break from the fast pace of city living. providing locals and visitors alike with opportunities for relaxation, recreation, and rejuvenation. Let's delve into six must-see city parks and urban green spaces in Milan, each offering a unique experience amidst nature's embrace.

Parco Sempione

Located in the center of Milan, Parco Sempione is an extensive urban park that spans over 47 acres, offering a tranquil retreat amidst the city's bustling streets. Located adjacent to the historic Sforza Castle, Parco Sempione is easily accessible by public transportation, with nearby metro and tram stops. Parco Sempione is open daily from dawn to dusk, allowing visitors to enjoy its lush landscapes, scenic ponds, and shaded pathways throughout the day. Entry to the park is free, making it a popular destination for locals and tourists seeking outdoor recreation and relaxation.

With its expansive lawns, picturesque gardens, and towering trees, Parco Sempione is the perfect spot for picnics, leisurely strolls, and outdoor activities. Visitors can also explore cultural attractions within the park, including the Triennale di Milano and the Arena Civica, which host exhibitions, concerts, and events throughout the year.

Giardini Pubblici Indro Montanelli
Located in the heart of Milan's historic district, the Giardini Pubblici Indro Montanelli is a beloved urban oasis that dates back to the 18th century. Named after the renowned journalist and writer Indro Montanelli, the park is easily reachable by public transportation, with nearby metro and tram stations.

The Giardini Pubblici Indro Montanelli is open daily from early morning until evening, providing visitors with ample opportunities to explore its verdant lawns, tranquil ponds, and botanical gardens. Entry to the park is free, making it accessible to all. This historic park holds cultural significance as one of Milan's oldest green spaces, providing a peaceful retreat for residents and visitors alike. Visitors can enjoy leisurely walks, admire seasonal blooms, and relax in shaded groves, away from the city's hustle and bustle. Additionally, the park is home to the Natural History Museum of Milan, where visitors can learn about the region's flora and fauna through interactive exhibits and displays.

Orto Botanico di Brera
Tucked away in Milan's historic Brera district, the Orto Botanico di Brera is a hidden gem that delights visitors with its botanical wonders and serene ambiance. Established in the 18th century, this botanical garden is dedicated to the study and conservation of plant species from around the world. The Orto Botanico di Brera is open to the public on select days, typically from Tuesday to Sunday, with varying opening hours depending on

the season. Admission fees may apply, with discounts available for students, seniors, and groups.

Visitors to the Orto Botanico di Brera can explore its diverse collection of plants, including rare and exotic specimens, arranged in thematic gardens and greenhouses. Guided tours and educational programs offer insight into the garden's scientific research and conservation efforts, making it an enriching destination for nature lovers and botany enthusiasts.

Parco delle Cave
For nature enthusiasts seeking a tranquil escape from the city's urban sprawl, Parco delle Cave offers a peaceful retreat amidst natural landscapes and biodiversity. Located on the outskirts of Milan, this expansive park encompasses former quarries, wetlands, and woodlands, providing habitat for diverse plant and animal species.

Parco delle Cave is open to the public year-round, with varying opening hours depending on the season. Visitors can access the park by car or public transportation, with nearby bus stops and parking facilities available. Entry to Parco delle Cave is free, allowing visitors to explore its network of walking and cycling trails, birdwatching areas, and scenic viewpoints. The park's natural beauty and ecological significance make it an ideal destination for outdoor activities such as hiking, nature photography, and environmental education.

Parco Nord Milano
Stretching across the northern outskirts of Milan, Parco Nord Milano is one of the largest urban parks in Europe, offering vast expanses of greenery, recreational facilities, and natural habitats. Spanning over 600 hectares, this expansive park is a haven for outdoor enthusiasts and nature lovers.

Parco Nord Milano is open daily, with extensive hours allowing visitors to enjoy its amenities from dawn to dusk. The park is accessible by public transportation, with nearby metro and bus stations providing convenient access for visitors. Entry to Parco Nord Milano is free, making it a popular destination for families, joggers, cyclists, and nature enthusiasts. The park features a wide range of recreational facilities, including sports fields, playgrounds, and picnic areas, as well as ecological zones, lakes, and wetlands that support diverse wildlife.

Boscoincittà

Located in the eastern outskirts of Milan, Boscoincittà is a unique urban forest that offers visitors a peaceful retreat amidst wooded landscapes, meadows, and nature trails. Spanning over 110 hectares, this expansive green space is an oasis of biodiversity and tranquility within the city limits.

Boscoincittà is open to the public year-round, with varying opening hours depending on the season. Visitors can access the park by car, bicycle, or public transportation, with nearby bus stops and parking facilities available. Entry to Boscoincittà is free, inviting visitors to explore its network of walking and cycling trails, birdwatching areas, and botanical gardens. The park's natural beauty and ecological significance make it an ideal destination for outdoor activities such as hiking, nature photography, and environmental education.

The city parks and green areas of Milan provide visitors with a refreshing escape from the bustling streets of the city, providing opportunities for relaxation, recreation, and connection with nature. Whether exploring historic gardens, wandering through wooded trails, or picnicking in lush meadows, visitors can immerse themselves in Milan's natural beauty and cultural heritage. So, whether you're seeking serenity amidst verdant landscapes or seeking adventure in the great outdoors, Milan's city parks and urban green spaces beckon with endless possibilities for exploration and enjoyment.

8.2 Cycling Routes and Bike Tours

Milan, known for its bustling streets and rich cultural heritage, also offers fantastic opportunities for cycling enthusiasts to explore the city's landmarks, parks, and hidden gems. With a network of well-maintained bike paths and guided tours, visitors can pedal their way through Milan's vibrant neighborhoods and iconic attractions. Let's delve into six must-see cycling routes and bike tours in Milan, each offering a unique perspective on the city's history, culture, and urban landscapes.

Navigli Canal District Bike Tour

Embark on a scenic bike tour through Milan's picturesque Navigli Canal District, where historic waterways and charming streets converge. Starting at the iconic Darsena, the city's historic dockyard, this guided tour takes cyclists along the scenic canals of Naviglio Grande and Naviglio Pavese, lined with quaint cafes, boutiques, and vibrant street art. The Navigli Canal District Bike Tour typically lasts 2-3 hours and is led by knowledgeable guides who provide insight into the area's history, architecture, and cultural significance. Cyclists can expect to pass by landmarks such as the Basilica di Sant'Eustorgio and the Vicolo dei Lavandai, a hidden gem known for its ancient washhouses.

The tour is suitable for cyclists of all levels and includes bike rental and safety equipment.Attendees are advised to bring water, sunscreen, and comfortable attire for the journey. Along the way, cyclists can stop to admire the scenery, take photos, and sample local delicacies at waterfront cafes, making it a memorable and immersive experience.

Milan City Center Bike Tour

Explore Milan's historic city center on a guided bike tour that showcases the city's iconic landmarks, majestic squares, and cultural treasures. Starting at Piazza del Duomo, cyclists pedal through the bustling streets of the fashion district, past elegant boutiques and designer showrooms, before reaching the grandeur of Sforza Castle and Parco Sempione.

The Milan City Center Bike Tour typically lasts 3-4 hours and covers approximately 10 kilometers of cycling through the city's vibrant neighborhoods. Led by experienced guides, the tour offers insights into Milan's rich history, from its medieval origins to its modern-day significance as a global fashion and design capital.

Bike rental and safety equipment are provided as part of the tour package, ensuring a comfortable and enjoyable experience for participants. Cyclists can expect to see highlights such as the La Scala Opera House, Galleria Vittorio Emanuele II, and the historic Brera district, with opportunities to stop for photos and refreshments along the way.

Milan Parklands Cycling Route
Escape the urban hustle and bustle on a leisurely cycling route through Milan's lush parklands and green spaces, where nature reigns supreme amidst the city's concrete jungle. Starting at Parco Sempione, cyclists pedal along tree-lined pathways, past tranquil ponds and manicured gardens, before reaching the expansive Parco Nord Milano.

The Milan Parklands Cycling Route offers cyclists a chance to explore the city's diverse ecosystems and biodiversity, from the wooded trails of Boscoincittà to the meadows of Parco Lambro. With designated bike paths and well-marked routes, cyclists can navigate the parklands with ease, enjoying the sights and sounds of nature along the way. This self-guided cycling route is suitable for cyclists of all ages and fitness levels, with options for shorter loops or longer excursions depending on individual preferences. Bike rental facilities are available at various locations throughout the city, with options for traditional bikes, electric bikes, and tandem bicycles.

Historical Milan Bike Tour
Step back in time on a historical bike tour of Milan, where centuries of art, architecture, and culture come to life amidst the city's storied streets and landmarks. Starting at the imposing Milan Cathedral, cyclists pedal through the medieval alleys of the Brera district, past ancient churches, palaces, and hidden courtyards. Led by expert guides, the Historical Milan Bike Tour offers insights into the city's rich heritage, from its Roman

origins to its Renaissance splendor and beyond. Cyclists can expect to see highlights such as the Church of Santa Maria delle Grazie, home to Leonardo da Vinci's masterpiece "The Last Supper," and the historic Navigli Canal District.

Bike rental and safety equipment are provided as part of the tour package, ensuring a comfortable and secure experience for participants. Along the way, cyclists can pause to explore landmarks, learn about Milan's history, and sample local cuisine at traditional trattorias, making it a memorable journey through time.

Milan Countryside Cycling Excursion

Venture beyond the city limits on a countryside cycling excursion that showcases the natural beauty and rural charm of Milan's surrounding countryside. Starting from the city center, cyclists pedal through scenic vineyards, rolling hills, and picturesque villages, immersing themselves in the idyllic landscapes of Lombardy. Led by experienced guides, the Milan Countryside Cycling Excursion offers opportunities for leisurely rides, wine tastings, and farm-to-table dining experiences at local agriturismi. Cyclists can explore charming towns such as Monza, known for its historic royal palace and lush parklands, or Bergamo, with its ancient city walls and panoramic vistas. Bike rental, transportation, and refreshments are included as part of the excursion package, ensuring a seamless and enjoyable experience for participants. Whether cycling through sun-dappled vineyards or savoring regional delicacies, this countryside excursion offers a refreshing escape from the urban hustle and bustle of Milan.

River Ticino Cycling Trail

Follow the scenic River Ticino on a cycling trail that winds through picturesque landscapes, charming villages, and historic landmarks in the Lombardy region. Starting from Milan, cyclists pedal along the riverbanks, past medieval castles, Romanesque churches, and verdant vineyards, soaking in the beauty of the Italian countryside.

The River Ticino Cycling Trail offers cyclists a chance to explore off-the-beaten-path destinations, from the medieval town of Vigevano with its majestic Piazza Ducale to the quaint village of Pavia, home to one of Italy's oldest universities. With well-marked trails and gentle terrain, the trail is suitable for cyclists of all levels and ages. Bike rental, maps, and accommodations are available along the trail, making it easy for cyclists to plan their journey and enjoy a memorable cycling adventure through the heart of Lombardy.Whether you're discovering historic landmarks, indulging in local cuisine, or savoring the serenity of nature, the River Ticino Cycling Trail offers a rewarding experience for cyclists seeking adventure and exploration.

Milan's cycling routes and bike tours offer visitors a unique and immersive way to explore the city's rich history, culture, and natural landscapes. Whether pedaling through historic neighborhoods, scenic parklands, or charming countryside, cyclists can experience Milan from a new perspective, discovering hidden gems and iconic landmarks along the way. With guided tours, self-guided routes, and excursions to suit every preference and skill level, Milan's cycling offerings cater to both leisure cyclists and avid adventurers alike, inviting visitors to saddle up and embark on an unforgettable journey through this vibrant and dynamic city.

8.3 Day Trips to Lakes Como and Maggiore

Milan, situated in the heart of Lombardy, offers not only its own cultural riches but also serves as a gateway to some of Italy's most enchanting destinations. From the serene beauty of Lake Como to the majestic allure of Lake Maggiore, there are countless day trips and excursions from Milan that promise unforgettable experiences. Let's delve into six must-see attractions near Milan, each offering a unique blend of natural beauty, historical significance, and cultural charm.

Lake Como

Nestled at the foothills of the Alps, Lake Como is a breathtaking destination renowned for its scenic landscapes, charming towns, and luxurious villas. Located approximately 50 kilometers north of Milan, Lake Como is easily accessible by train or car, with frequent services departing from Milan's central station.

Visitors to Lake Como can explore picturesque towns such as Bellagio, Varenna, and Menaggio, each offering its own unique blend of history, culture, and natural beauty. Stroll along the lakefront promenades, visit historic landmarks such as Villa del Balbianello and Villa Carlotta, or embark on a scenic boat cruise to admire the stunning views of the surrounding mountains and shoreline. Entry to most lakeside attractions may require a fee, but simply wandering through the charming streets and enjoying the breathtaking scenery is free of charge. Lake Como's tranquil ambiance and timeless allure make it a must-visit destination for travelers seeking relaxation, romance, and inspiration amidst nature's splendor.

Lake Maggiore
Situated to the west of Milan, Lake Maggiore is another captivating destination known for its crystal-clear waters, lush gardens, and historic palaces. Accessible from Milan by train or car, Lake Maggiore offers a tranquil escape from the city, with charming towns and verdant landscapes waiting to be explored.

The Borromean Islands, located in the middle of Lake Maggiore, are a major highlight of any visit to the region. Visitors can tour the opulent palaces and manicured gardens of Isola Bella and Isola Madre, or explore the quaint streets of the fishing village on Isola dei Pescatori. Ferry services operate regularly from Stresa, Baveno, and other lakeside towns, providing easy access to the Borromean Islands and other attractions. While there may be entry fees for certain attractions, the natural beauty and cultural heritage of Lake Maggiore are priceless, offering visitors an unforgettable day of exploration and relaxation.

Bergamo
Located just 50 kilometers northeast of Milan, Bergamo is a charming medieval city characterized by its ancient walls, cobblestone streets, and historic landmarks. Divided into two distinct areas – the Upper Town (Città Alta) and the Lower Town (Città Bassa) – Bergamo offers visitors a glimpse into Italy's rich history and cultural heritage.

To reach Bergamo from Milan, travelers can take a direct train or bus, with journey times of approximately one hour. Upon arrival, visitors can explore the Upper Town's medieval fortress, Piazza Vecchia, and the stunning Basilica of Santa Maria Maggiore, adorned with exquisite Renaissance frescoes. Entry to historical sites such as the Rocca di Bergamo and the Accademia Carrara may require a fee, but wandering through the city's atmospheric streets and enjoying panoramic views of the surrounding countryside is free of charge. Bergamo's timeless charm and architectural beauty make it a delightful day trip destination for history enthusiasts and culture seekers alike.

Verona

Famous as the setting of Shakespeare's Romeo and Juliet, Verona is a romantic city steeped in history, art, and culture. Located approximately 160 kilometers east of Milan, Verona can be reached by train in under two hours, making it an ideal day trip destination for travelers seeking a taste of Italian romance.

Upon arrival in Verona, visitors can explore the city's UNESCO-listed historic center, which boasts landmarks such as the Arena di Verona, a well-preserved Roman amphitheater, and the medieval Castelvecchio fortress. Don't miss the chance to visit Juliet's House (Casa di Giulietta), where visitors can see Juliet's balcony and leave love notes on the walls. Entry fees may apply for certain attractions in Verona, but simply wandering through the city's ancient streets, sampling local cuisine, and soaking up the romantic atmosphere is free of charge. Verona's timeless beauty and cultural significance make it a must-visit destination for travelers seeking romance, history, and art.

Lake Garda

Located just 100 kilometers east of Milan, Lake Garda is Italy's largest lake and a popular destination for outdoor enthusiasts, nature lovers, and culture seekers. Accessible by train, bus, or car, Lake Garda offers a diverse range of attractions, from charming lakeside towns to scenic hiking trails and historic landmarks.

Visitors to Lake Garda can explore picturesque towns such as Sirmione, Bardolino, and Malcesine, each boasting its distinctive fusion of history, culture, and natural splendor. Don't miss the chance to visit the Scaligero Castle in Sirmione, ride the cable car to the top of Monte Baldo for panoramic views of the lake, or relax on the shores of Garda's sandy beaches. While there may be entry fees for certain attractions and activities, simply enjoying the stunning scenery and serene ambiance of Lake Garda is free of charge. Whether hiking in the mountains, sailing on the lake, or exploring historic towns, Lake Garda offers endless opportunities for adventure and relaxation.

Pavia

Located approximately 35 kilometers south of Milan, Pavia is a charming medieval town known for its historic university, ancient churches, and tranquil riverfront. Accessible by train or car, Pavia offers visitors a peaceful retreat from the hustle and bustle of the city, with well-preserved architecture and cultural landmarks waiting to be explored.

Upon arrival in Pavia, visitors can explore the historic center's cobblestone streets, visit the iconic Ponte Coperto bridge spanning the Ticino River, and admire the stunning interior of the Certosa di Pavia, a magnificent Carthusian monastery. Entry fees may apply for certain attractions in Pavia, but simply wandering through the town's atmospheric streets, sampling local cuisine, and enjoying views of the riverfront is free of charge. Pavia's rich history, cultural heritage, and relaxed pace make it a delightful day trip destination for travelers seeking tranquility and charm.

Milan's proximity to some of Italy's most enchanting destinations makes it an ideal base for day trips and excursions. From the serene beauty of Lake Como and Lake Maggiore to the historic charm of Bergamo and Verona, there are endless opportunities for exploration and discovery just a short distance from the city. Whether seeking natural beauty, cultural heritage, or romantic charm, these day trips from Milan offer something for every traveler, promising unforgettable experiences and memories to last a lifetime.

8.4 Hiking in the Lombardy Region

The Lombardy region, with its diverse landscapes ranging from majestic mountains to serene lakeshores, offers a plethora of hiking opportunities for outdoor enthusiasts. Just a short distance from Milan, visitors can escape the urban hustle and bustle and immerse themselves in nature's beauty through various hiking trails and activities. Let's delve into six must-see hiking activities in Lombardy, each offering a unique blend of natural wonders, cultural heritage, and outdoor adventure.

Lake Como Greenway

Located approximately 50 kilometers north of Milan, Lake Como is surrounded by a network of scenic hiking trails known as the Lake Como Greenway. Stretching over 10 kilometers, the Greenway connects the charming towns of Colonno and Griante, offering breathtaking views of the lake and surrounding mountains. The Lake Como Greenway is open year-round, with varying trail conditions depending on the season. Visitors can access the trail by public transportation or car, with designated parking areas available in nearby towns.

There is no entry fee to hike the Lake Como Greenway, making it accessible to all. Along the trail, hikers can explore historic villas, lush gardens, and quaint villages, as well as enjoy picnics by the lake and swimming in designated areas.

Monte Grona

For more experienced hikers seeking a challenge, Monte Grona offers a rewarding ascent with panoramic views of Lake Como and the surrounding Alps. Located near Menaggio, approximately 70 kilometers north of Milan, Monte Grona is accessible via well-marked hiking trails.

The ascent to Monte Grona typically takes 4-6 hours round trip, depending on the chosen route and hiker's pace. Visitors can reach the trailhead by public transportation or car, with parking available at designated areas near the trailhead. There is no entry fee to hike Monte Grona, but visitors should be prepared with appropriate hiking gear, including sturdy footwear, water, and snacks. Along the way, hikers can enjoy stunning views of Lake Como, alpine meadows, and rugged mountain landscapes.

Val Grande National Park

Located approximately 150 kilometers northwest of Milan, Val Grande National Park is Italy's largest wilderness area, offering remote hiking trails and pristine natural beauty. Accessible from the town of Verbania, Val Grande is a haven for outdoor enthusiasts seeking solitude and adventure. The hiking trails in Val Grande National Park vary in difficulty and length, ranging from short day hikes to multi-day treks. Visitors can access the park by car or public transportation, with trailheads located in nearby villages such as Cicogna and Rovegro.

There is no entry fee to access Val Grande National Park, but visitors should be prepared for rugged terrain and remote conditions. Hikers can explore ancient beech forests, alpine meadows, and rugged peaks, as well as spot wildlife such as chamois, ibex, and golden eagles.

Valsassina

Located approximately 60 kilometers northeast of Milan, Valsassina is a picturesque valley nestled between the Grigna and Resegone mountain ranges, offering a variety of hiking trails for all skill levels. Accessible by car or public transportation, Valsassina is a popular destination for day trips and outdoor adventures. The hiking trails in Valsassina range from easy walks through alpine meadows to challenging ascents to mountain peaks. Visitors can explore the valley's charming villages, such as Barzio and Pasturo, or venture into the surrounding mountains for more rugged terrain.

There is no entry fee to hike in Valsassina, but visitors should be prepared for changing weather conditions and steep trails. Along the way, hikers can enjoy stunning views of the valley below, as well as spot wildlife such as deer, marmots, and alpine ibex.

Monte Resegone

For adventurous hikers seeking a challenging ascent, Monte Resegone offers a rewarding climb with panoramic views of the Lombardy region. Located approximately 60 kilometers northeast of Milan, Monte Resegone is accessible via well-marked hiking trails from the town of Lecco.

The ascent to Monte Resegone typically takes 4-6 hours round trip, depending on the chosen route and hiker's pace. Visitors can reach the trailhead by car or public transportation, with parking available at designated areas near the trailhead. There is no entry fee to hike Monte Resegone, but visitors should be prepared with appropriate hiking gear, including sturdy footwear, water, and snacks. Along the way, hikers can enjoy sweeping views of Lake Como, the Alps, and the Po Valley, as well as explore the mountain's rugged terrain and rocky peaks.

Sentiero del Viandante

Stretching along the eastern shore of Lake Como, the Sentiero del Viandante is a historic hiking trail that offers stunning views of the lake and surrounding mountains. Accessible from various towns along the eastern shore, including Varenna and Bellano, the Sentiero del Viandante is a popular destination for day hikes and multi-day treks. The hiking trail is open year-round, with varying trail conditions depending on the season. Visitors can access the trail by public transportation or car, with designated parking areas available in nearby towns.

There is no entry fee to hike the Sentiero del Viandante, making it accessible to all. Along the trail, hikers can explore historic villages, ancient Roman roads, and picturesque landscapes, as well as enjoy picnics by the lake and swimming in designated areas. Lombardy region offers a wealth of hiking opportunities for outdoor enthusiasts, from scenic lakeside trails to rugged mountain ascents. Whether exploring the shores of Lake Como, venturing into the wilderness of Val Grande National Park, or climbing the peaks of Monte Resegone, there is something

8.5 Sports Events and Activities

Milan also offers a wide range of sports events and activities for visitors to enjoy. From world-class football matches to adrenaline-pumping outdoor adventures, Milan has something to offer sports enthusiasts of all ages and interests. Let's delve into six must-see sports events and activities in Milan, each providing a unique experience that showcases the city's dynamic energy and passion for sports.

AC Milan and Inter Milan Football Matches

Located at the iconic San Siro Stadium, AC Milan and Inter Milan, two of Italy's most successful football clubs, regularly host thrilling matches that attract fans from around the world. The San Siro Stadium, also known as the Stadio Giuseppe Meazza, is located in the San Siro district of Milan and is easily accessible by public transportation.

Football matches are typically held on weekends and occasionally on weekdays, with varying kickoff times depending on the schedule. Tickets to AC Milan and Inter Milan matches can be purchased online through the clubs' official websites or at ticket booths located outside the stadium on match days. Witnessing a football match at the San Siro Stadium is a remarkable experience for sports fans, offering the chance to witness the passion and excitement of Italian football firsthand. Visitors can soak up the electric atmosphere of the stadium, cheer on their favorite teams, and immerse themselves in Milan's football culture.

Cycling along the Navigli Canals

For a leisurely and scenic sports activity, cycling along the Navigli canals offers a unique way to explore Milan's historic waterways and vibrant neighborhoods. The Navigli district is located in the heart of Milan and is easily accessible by bike rental or by bringing your own bicycle. The Navigli canals are open to cyclists year-round, providing a picturesque route that winds through charming streets, bustling markets, and historic landmarks. Cyclists can rent bicycles from various rental shops located throughout the city or join guided cycling tours that explore the Navigli district and other scenic areas of Milan.

Cycling along the Navigli canals allows visitors to enjoy the beauty of Milan's waterways while getting some exercise and fresh air. Along the way, cyclists can stop at cafes, restaurants, and artisan shops to sample local cuisine and soak up the atmosphere of this lively district.

Running in Parco Sempione

Parco Sempione, Milan's largest public park, offers an ideal setting for outdoor running and jogging amidst lush greenery and scenic landscapes. Located near the historic center of Milan, Parco Sempione is easily accessible by public transportation or on foot. The park is open daily from dawn until dusk, providing ample opportunities for runners to enjoy their workout in a peaceful and natural environment. There is no entry fee to access Parco Sempione, making it a popular destination for locals and visitors alike.

Running in Parco Sempione allows visitors to escape the hustle and bustle of the city and enjoy a refreshing workout surrounded by nature. The park features well-maintained paths, shaded trails, and open spaces where runners can tailor their workout to their preferences and fitness levels.

Tennis at Foro Italico

Foro Italico, located in the Portello district of Milan, is a sprawling sports complex that offers a variety of recreational activities, including tennis courts that are open to the public. The complex is easily accessible by public transportation or car, with parking available onsite.

Tennis courts at Foro Italico can be reserved in advance online or by phone, with hourly rental rates varying depending on the time of day and day of the week. Visitors can bring their own equipment or rent tennis rackets and balls onsite for an additional fee. Playing tennis at Foro Italico provides visitors with the opportunity to enjoy a fun and active sports activity while soaking up the sun and fresh air. The complex also offers other amenities such as swimming pools, gyms, and sports fields, making it a comprehensive destination for fitness enthusiasts.

Skateboarding at Bastioni di Porta Venezia

Bastioni di Porta Venezia, located in the heart of Milan's Porta Venezia district, is a popular spot for skateboarders to practice their skills and enjoy the thrill of outdoor skating. The skatepark is easily accessible by public transportation or on foot, with plenty of space for parking nearby.

The skatepark is open to the public year-round, providing a safe and welcoming environment for skaters of all ages and skill levels. There is no entry fee to access Bastioni di Porta Venezia, making it a budget-friendly option for sports enthusiasts. Skateboarding at Bastioni di Porta Venezia allows visitors to join a vibrant community of skaters and enjoy the freedom of expression that comes with this dynamic sport. The skatepark features ramps, rails, and obstacles where skaters can practice tricks and hone their skills in a supportive atmosphere.

Golfing at Golf Club Milano

For golf enthusiasts looking to indulge in a round of golf amidst scenic landscapes and lush greenery, Golf Club Milano offers an exclusive and challenging course just outside the city center. Located in the small town of Barlassina, approximately 20 kilometers north of Milan, Golf Club Milano is accessible by car or public transportation.

The golf course at Golf Club Milano is open year-round, weather permitting, with tee times available throughout the day. Visitors can book tee times in advance online or by phone, with green fees varying depending on the time of day and day of the week. Golfing at Golf Club Milano provides visitors with the opportunity to enjoy a leisurely and invigorating sports activity while surrounded by natural beauty. The course features 18 holes set amidst rolling hills, wooded areas,

8.6 Family and Kids Friendly Activities

Milan also offers a plethora of family-friendly activities and attractions that cater to visitors of all ages. From interactive museums to expansive parks and thrilling amusement parks, there's no shortage of fun-filled adventures for families to enjoy in this vibrant city. Let's delve into six must-see family and kid-friendly activities in Milan, each promising an unforgettable experience that will delight both children and adults alike.

Leonardo da Vinci National Museum of Science and Technology

Located in the heart of Milan, the Leonardo da Vinci National Museum of Science and Technology is an educational and entertaining destination for families with children of all ages. The museum is housed in a historic monastery complex, providing a unique setting for exploring the wonders of science and technology.

The museum is open from Tuesday to Sunday, with varying hours depending on the season. Admission fees apply, with discounted rates available for children, families, and groups. Visitors can reach the museum by public transportation or car, with parking available nearby. The Leonardo da Vinci National Museum of Science and Technology offers a wide range of interactive exhibits, workshops, and hands-on activities that engage and inspire young minds. From exploring Leonardo da Vinci's inventions to learning about space exploration and robotics, there's something for everyone to enjoy at this fascinating museum.

Parco Giochi Cavallino Rosso (Red Pony Park)

Parco Giochi Cavallino Rosso, also known as Red Pony Park, is a charming amusement park located in the outskirts of Milan. Nestled amidst lush greenery and scenic landscapes, the park offers a range of rides, attractions, and activities that are suitable for children of all ages. The park is open daily during the summer months and on weekends during the rest of the year. Admission fees apply, with discounted rates available for children and families. Visitors can reach the park by car or public transportation, with parking available onsite.

Red Pony Park features a variety of rides and attractions, including carousels, bumper cars, mini-golf, and a petting zoo. Families can also enjoy picnics in the park's spacious picnic areas or indulge in delicious treats at the park's snack bars and cafes.

Acquaworld Water Park

Located in the nearby town of Concorezzo, just a short drive from Milan, Acquaworld Water Park is a thrilling destination for families seeking fun and excitement. The water park features a wide range of slides, pools, and water attractions that cater to visitors of all ages and swimming abilities. Acquaworld Water Park is open daily during the summer months and on weekends during the rest of the year. Admission fees apply, with discounted rates available for children, families, and groups. Visitors can reach the water park by car or public transportation, with parking available onsite.

The water park offers a variety of attractions, including wave pools, lazy rivers, and adrenaline-pumping slides. Families can also relax in the park's sun lounges, enjoy refreshments at the snack bars, or participate in aqua fitness classes and swimming lessons.

Parco Sempione and Sempione Park Playground

Parco Sempione, Milan's largest public park, is a fantastic destination for families to enjoy outdoor activities and recreation amidst lush greenery and scenic landscapes. Located near the historic center of Milan, Parco Sempione is easily accessible by public transportation or on foot. The park is open daily from dawn until dusk, with no admission fee required for entry. Families can reach the park by public transportation or car, with parking available in nearby areas.

Parco Sempione features a dedicated playground area for children, complete with swings, slides, climbing structures, and sandboxes. Families can also enjoy picnics in the park's spacious picnic areas, rent bicycles for leisurely rides, or explore the park's historic landmarks and monuments.

MUBA - Children's Museum of Milan

MUBA, the Children's Museum of Milan, is a vibrant and interactive museum dedicated to providing educational and creative experiences for children and families. Located in the historic Palazzo della Ragione, MUBA offers a range of exhibitions, workshops, and activities that encourage exploration, imagination, and learning.

The museum is open from Tuesday to Sunday, with varying hours depending on the season. Admission fees apply, with discounted rates available for children, families, and groups. Visitors can reach the museum by public transportation or on foot, with parking available nearby. MUBA features a variety of interactive exhibits and play areas that cater to children of all ages, from toddlers to teenagers. Families can explore themed galleries, participate in art workshops, and attend storytelling sessions, making it a dynamic and engaging destination for creative play and discovery.

Giardini Pubblici Indro Montanelli (Indro Montanelli Public Gardens)
Giardini Pubblici Indro Montanelli, also known as Indro Montanelli Public Gardens, is a tranquil oasis located in the heart of Milan. The gardens offer a peaceful retreat from the bustling city streets, with lush green lawns, shady trees, and scenic pathways.

The gardens are open daily from dawn until dusk, with no admission fee required for entry. Families can reach the gardens by public transportation or on foot, with parking available in nearby areas.

Indro Montanelli Public Gardens features a playground area for children, as well as a small zoo with a variety of animals, including deer, peacocks, and turtles. Families can also enjoy picnics on the lawns, rent pedal boats on the lake, or visit the Natural History Museum located within the gardens.

8.7 Activities for Solo Travelers
Solo travelers seeking adventure, culture, and exploration will find Milan to be a captivating destination filled with a variety of activities to enjoy alone. From wandering through historic neighborhoods to savoring culinary delights, Milan offers endless opportunities for solo exploration and discovery. Let's explore six must-see activities for

solo travelers in Milan, each offering a unique experience that celebrates the city's rich heritage and vibrant energy.

Explore the Historic Center of Milan

Located in the heart of the city, the historic center of Milan is a treasure trove of architectural wonders, cultural landmarks, and hidden gems waiting to be discovered. Solo travelers can wander through narrow cobblestone streets, admire centuries-old buildings, and soak up the atmosphere of this bustling district.

The historic center is open to explore at any time of day, with many attractions offering extended hours for visitors. There is no entry fee to explore the historic center, making it accessible to all travelers. Visitors can reach the area by public transportation, taxi, or on foot, with parking available in nearby garages. Exploring the historic center of Milan allows solo travelers to immerse themselves in the city's rich history and cultural heritage. From marveling at the Gothic grandeur of the Duomo di Milano to browsing the shops along the fashionable Via Montenapoleone, there's plenty to see and do in this vibrant district.

Visit the Pinacoteca di Brera

For art lovers and solo travelers seeking cultural enrichment, a visit to the Pinacoteca di Brera is a must. Located in the Brera district of Milan, this renowned art gallery is home to a remarkable array of Italian masterpieces, encompassing creations by Caravaggio, Raphael, and Titian.

The Pinacoteca di Brera is open from Tuesday to Sunday, with varying hours depending on the day. Admission fees apply, with discounted rates available for solo travelers, students, and seniors. Visitors can reach the gallery by public transportation or on foot, with parking available nearby. A visit to the Pinacoteca di Brera offers solo travelers the opportunity to admire some of Italy's most celebrated artworks in a tranquil and intimate setting. From Renaissance masterpieces to Baroque treasures, the gallery's diverse collection provides a fascinating glimpse into the country's artistic heritage.

Take a Food Tour of Milan

For solo travelers with a passion for food and culinary exploration, a food tour of Milan offers the perfect opportunity to sample the city's diverse and delicious cuisine. Guided food tours take visitors on a culinary journey through Milan's neighborhoods, where they can taste authentic Italian dishes and learn about the city's gastronomic traditions.

Food tours are available throughout the day and evening, with options to suit every taste and budget. Prices vary depending on the tour provider and the length of the tour. Solo travelers can book food tours online in advance or join a group tour upon arrival in Milan A food tour of Milan allows solo travelers to discover hidden gems and local favorites, from bustling markets and traditional trattorias to trendy cafes and gourmet restaurants. Whether indulging in creamy risotto alla Milanese or savoring artisanal gelato, solo travelers are sure to delight their taste buds on a culinary adventure through Milan.

Take a Stroll along the Navigli Canals

For solo travelers seeking relaxation and serenity, a leisurely stroll along the Navigli canals offers a scenic escape from the hustle and bustle of the city. The Navigli district is located in the southern part of Milan and is known for its picturesque waterways, charming cafes, and vibrant nightlife.

The Navigli canals are open to explore at any time of day, with many cafes and bars offering outdoor seating along the waterfront. There is no entry fee to visit the Navigli district, making it a budget-friendly option for solo travelers. Visitors can reach the area by public transportation, taxi, or on foot, with parking available in nearby garages. Taking a stroll along the Navigli canals allows solo travelers to soak up the atmosphere of this lively district, where historic bridges, colorful buildings, and bustling markets line the waterfront. From browsing vintage shops and artisan boutiques to enjoying aperitivo hour at a local bar, there's plenty to see and do along the Navigli canals.

Attend a Performance at Teatro alla Scala

For solo travelers with a love for the performing arts, attending a performance at Teatro alla Scala is a cultural experience not to be missed. Located in the heart of Milan, Teatro alla Scala is one of the world's most famous opera houses, renowned for its rich history, stunning architecture, and world-class performances. Teatro alla Scala offers performances throughout the year, including opera, ballet, and classical music concerts. Ticket prices vary depending on the performance and seating location, with discounts available for solo travelers, students, and seniors. Visitors can purchase tickets online in advance or at the box office on the day of the performance.

Attending a performance at Teatro alla Scala allows solo travelers to immerse themselves in the beauty and drama of Italian opera and ballet. From the opulent interiors of the theater to the exquisite performances on stage, a night at Teatro alla Scala is sure to be a memorable highlight of any trip to Milan.

Relax in Parco Sempione

For solo travelers seeking tranquility and natural beauty, Parco Sempione offers a peaceful oasis in the heart of Milan. This expansive public park is located near the historic center of the city and is perfect for leisurely walks, picnics, and relaxation. Parco Sempione is open daily from dawn until dusk, with no entry fee required for entry. Visitors can reach the park by public transportation, taxi, or on foot, with parking available in nearby areas. The park features lush green lawns, shady trees, and scenic pathways, providing the perfect escape from the city's hustle and bustle.

Relaxing in Parco Sempione allows solo travelers to unwind and recharge amidst natural beauty and tranquil surroundings. From enjoying a picnic by the lake to taking a leisurely stroll through the park's gardens, there are plenty of ways to relax and enjoy the serenity of Parco Sempione.

CHAPTER 9

SHOPPING IN MILAN

Click the link or Scan QR Code with a device to view a comprehensive map of Shopping Options in Milan – https://shorturl.at/beIF6

9.1 Fashion Districts and Luxury Boutiques

Milan, the epitome of style and sophistication, is home to several renowned fashion districts and luxury boutiques that attract fashion enthusiasts from around the globe. From the historic Quadrilatero della Moda to the trendy streets of Brera, each district offers a distinct shopping experience, showcasing the latest trends and designer collections. Here, we delve into six of Milan's most iconic fashion districts and luxury boutiques, highlighting their unique offerings and attractions.

Quadrilatero della Moda: Located in the heart of Milan, the Quadrilatero della Moda, or Fashion Quadrangle, is synonymous with luxury and opulence. This prestigious district is home to some of the world's most prestigious fashion houses, including Prada, Gucci, Versace, and Dolce & Gabbana. Visitors can explore flagship stores and boutiques showcasing the latest haute couture collections, exquisite accessories, and iconic leather goods. Prices in this district tend to be high, reflecting the quality and craftsmanship associated with luxury brands. Most stores in the Quadrilatero della Moda are open from 10:00 AM to 7:00 PM, Monday to Saturday, and can be easily reached via public transportation, with the Montenapoleone metro station nearby.

Brera: Nestled in Milan's artistic and bohemian quarter, the Brera district exudes a chic and eclectic vibe, making it a favorite destination for fashion-forward individuals. Here, visitors can discover a mix of luxury boutiques, independent designers, and trendy concept stores. From avant-garde fashion to unique accessories and artisanal crafts, Brera offers a diverse array of shopping options to suit every taste and budget. Prices may vary depending on the brand and the item's exclusivity, but overall, shoppers can expect to find high-quality products with a touch of Italian flair. Most stores in Brera operate from 11:00 AM to 8:00 PM, Monday to Saturday, and can be accessed via public transportation, with the Lanza metro station nearby.

Porta Ticinese: Situated near Milan's historic city center, Porta Ticinese is a bustling district known for its vibrant street fashion and eclectic shopping scene. Here, visitors can explore a mix of vintage boutiques, contemporary fashion stores, and bohemian markets, offering an array of unique finds at affordable prices. From retro-inspired clothing to handmade accessories and quirky home decor items, Porta Ticinese caters to fashion enthusiasts looking for distinctive pieces with a touch of urban edge. Prices in this district are generally lower compared to luxury boutiques, making it an ideal destination for budget-conscious shoppers. Most stores in Porta Ticinese are open from 10:00 AM to 8:00 PM, Monday to Saturday, and can be easily reached by tram or metro.

Corso Vittorio Emanuele II: As one of Milan's busiest shopping streets, Corso Vittorio Emanuele II offers a mix of high-end fashion brands, popular retailers, and luxury boutiques housed within elegant historic buildings. Visitors can stroll along this bustling thoroughfare and explore flagship stores from renowned designers such as Louis Vuitton, Burberry, and Armani. From designer handbags to premium footwear and ready-to-wear collections, Corso Vittorio Emanuele II boasts a wide range of luxury offerings to cater to discerning shoppers. Prices here vary depending on the brand and the item's exclusivity, with some stores offering mid-range options alongside high-end couture. Most stores along Corso Vittorio Emanuele II are open from 10:00 AM to 8:00 PM, Monday to Saturday, and can be accessed via public transportation, with the Duomo metro station nearby.

Via della Spiga: Adjacent to the famous Via Montenapoleone, Via della Spiga is another prestigious fashion destination renowned for its exclusive boutiques and designer labels. Here, visitors can peruse luxury stores from iconic brands such as Chanel, Prada, and Bottega Veneta, showcasing the latest runway collections and timeless classics. From elegant eveningwear to sophisticated accessories and coveted leather goods, Via della Spiga offers an unparalleled shopping experience for fashion connoisseurs. Prices in this district are typically high, reflecting the prestige and craftsmanship associated with luxury brands. Most stores along Via della Spiga operate from 10:00 AM to 7:00 PM, Monday to Saturday, and can be easily accessed via public transportation, with the Montenapoleone metro station nearby.

Navigli: Known for its picturesque canals and vibrant nightlife, the Navigli district also boasts a thriving fashion scene with an eclectic mix of boutiques, vintage stores, and artisan workshops.Visitors have the opportunity to wander through narrow cobblestone streets adorned with unique shops offering a diverse array of goods.from retro clothing and handmade jewelry to unique accessories and bohemian home decor. Prices in Navigli vary depending on the store and the item's uniqueness, offering something for every budget. Most shops in this district are open from 10:00 AM to 8:00 PM, Monday to Saturday, and can be reached via tram or metro, with several stations serving the area.

Milan's fashion districts and luxury boutiques offer a diverse array of shopping experiences, from the opulent boutiques of the Quadrilatero della Moda to the eclectic charm of Navigli. Whether you're seeking haute couture creations or unique artisanal finds, each district provides an exclusive ambiance and assortment to cater to even the most selective fashion enthusiasts. With convenient access to public transportation and a wealth of shopping options, Milan remains a premier destination for indulging in the world of fashion and style.

9.2 Vintage and Designer Thrift Stores

Milan, renowned as one of the fashion capitals of the world, offers a treasure trove of vintage and designer thrift stores for the discerning shopper. These boutiques not only offer unique pieces but also provide a glimpse into the rich fashion history of the city. Here, we delve into six notable vintage and designer thrift stores in Milan, each with its own distinctive charm and offerings.

Old Fashion Vintage Market: Nestled in the heart of Milan's bustling Navigli district, Old Fashion Vintage Market stands out as a haven for vintage enthusiasts. This sprawling store boasts a diverse collection of clothing, accessories, and home decor items spanning various eras. From elegant Victorian dresses to retro '80s jackets, the selection caters to a wide range of tastes. Prices are reasonable, with many items priced affordably, making it a budget-friendly option for shoppers. Old Fashion Vintage Market is open from 10:00 AM to 7:00 PM, Monday through Saturday. To get there, visitors can take the metro to the Porta Genova station and walk a short distance to the Navigli canals.

Cavalli e Nastri: Situated in the trendy Brera district, Cavalli e Nastri exudes old-world charm with its vintage ambiance and carefully curated collection. This boutique specializes in high-end vintage clothing and accessories from luxury designers such as Chanel, Yves Saint Laurent, and Gucci. While prices may be on the higher end, the quality and authenticity of the pieces justify the cost for many fashion aficionados. Cavalli e Nastri is open from 10:30 AM to 7:30 PM, Monday to Saturday, and is conveniently located near the Moscova metro station.

Humana Vintage: Located near Milan's bustling Corso Buenos Aires shopping street, Humana Vintage offers a vast selection of second-hand clothing and accessories at affordable prices. This spacious store features an eclectic mix of items, including retro dresses, vintage denim, and unique costume jewelry. Bargain hunters will appreciate the regular sales and discounts offered here. Humana Vintage operates from 10:00 AM to 8:00 PM, Monday to Saturday, making it easily accessible for shoppers exploring the city center.

Twice Boutique: Tucked away in the charming Brera district, Twice Boutique is a hidden gem for those seeking designer treasures at discounted prices. This upscale thrift store features carefully curated collections of pre-loved designer clothing, shoes, and accessories from brands like Prada, Dolce & Gabbana, and Versace. While prices may still reflect the quality and prestige of the brands, shoppers can expect significant savings compared to retail prices. Twice Boutique is open from 11:00 AM to 7:30 PM, Monday to Saturday, and is conveniently located near the Lanza metro station.

Vintage Delirium: Situated in Milan's vibrant Porta Ticinese district, Vintage Delirium beckons with its eclectic mix of vintage and designer pieces. From retro sunglasses to one-of-a-kind leather jackets, this boutique offers a diverse range of items to suit every style and budget. Prices vary depending on the rarity and condition of the pieces, but overall, Vintage Delirium provides excellent value for vintage enthusiasts. The store is open from 11:00 AM to 7:30 PM, Monday to Saturday, and can be easily reached via public transportation, with the Porta Genova metro station nearby.

Bivio Milano: Located in the bustling Isola district, Bivio Milano stands out for its unique blend of vintage finds and contemporary fashion. This eclectic store features an ever-changing selection of clothing, accessories, and home decor items sourced from both local artisans and international designers. While prices may vary depending on the item's origin and rarity, Bivio Milano offers something for every budget. The store is open from 10:00 AM to 8:00 PM, Monday to Saturday, and is conveniently located near the Zara metro station.

Milan's vintage and designer thrift stores offer a diverse array of treasures waiting to be discovered. Whether you're hunting for a vintage statement piece or a designer bargain, these boutiques provide an immersive shopping experience that celebrates the city's rich fashion heritage. From the bustling streets of Navigli to the chic boutiques of Brera, each store offers its own unique charm and selection, ensuring that every shopper finds something special to take home.

9.3 Artisanal Crafts and Souvenirs

Milan, renowned for its fashion and design, also offers a plethora of artisanal craft shops and souvenir boutiques, providing visitors with an opportunity to take home a piece of the city's rich cultural heritage. From handmade ceramics to traditional leather goods, these establishments showcase the skill and creativity of local artisans. Here, we delve into six distinctive artisanal craft shops and souvenir stores in Milan, each offering its own unique treasures and shopping experience.

Bottega del Duomo: Situated near Milan's iconic Duomo Cathedral, Bottega del Duomo is a charming shop dedicated to showcasing traditional Italian craftsmanship. Here, visitors can find a wide array of artisanal souvenirs, including hand-painted ceramics, leather goods, and intricate lacework. Prices vary depending on the item's intricacy and materials used, but overall, Bottega del Duomo offers quality products at reasonable prices. The shop is open from 9:30 AM to 7:30 PM, Monday to Sunday, making it easily accessible to tourists exploring the city center.

MERCATO DELLE PIAZZE: Located in the lively Piazza San Marco, MERCATO DELLE PIAZZE is a vibrant marketplace where visitors can discover a diverse selection of artisanal crafts and locally made products. From handmade jewelry and textiles to gourmet food items and organic skincare products, the market offers something for every taste and preference. Prices at MERCATO DELLE PIAZZE vary depending on the vendor and the item's uniqueness, with many products available at affordable prices. The market is open from 9:00 AM to 7:00 PM, Tuesday to Sunday, and can be accessed via public transportation, with several bus and tram stops nearby.

Ceramiche d'Arte: Tucked away in Milan's charming Brera district, Ceramiche d'Arte is a hidden gem for pottery enthusiasts seeking unique and handcrafted ceramics. This boutique studio showcases a wide range of ceramic creations, including decorative vases, dinnerware sets, and intricately designed tiles. Prices at Ceramiche d'Arte vary depending on the size and complexity of the piece, with some items priced affordably for budget-conscious shoppers. The studio is open from 10:00 AM to 7:00 PM, Monday to Saturday, and can be reached on foot or by public transportation, with the Lanza metro station nearby.

La Bottega dei Mascareri: Located near Milan's famous Teatro alla Scala, La Bottega dei Mascareri specializes in traditional Venetian masks and masquerade accessories.

Visitors can browse a fascinating array of handcrafted masks, each meticulously crafted using traditional techniques passed down through generations. Prices for masks at La Bottega dei Mascareri vary depending on the design, materials, and level of detail, with some exquisite pieces commanding higher prices. The shop is open from 10:00 AM to 7:00 PM, Monday to Saturday, and is conveniently located within walking distance of the Duomo metro station.

Artigianato e Tradizione: Situated in Milan's historic Navigli district, Artigianato e Tradizione celebrates the city's artisanal heritage with a curated selection of handmade crafts and traditional souvenirs. Here, visitors can find an eclectic mix of products, including handmade leather goods, hand-painted ceramics, and locally sourced textiles. Prices at Artigianato e Tradizione vary depending on the item's craftsmanship and materials, with many affordable options available for souvenir seekers. The shop is open from 10:00 AM to 8:00 PM, Monday to Saturday, and can be accessed by tram or metro, with several stations serving the Navigli area.

Antica Cartoleria: Nestled in Milan's picturesque Brera district, Antica Cartoleria is a charming stationery shop specializing in artisanal paper goods and writing instruments. Visitors can peruse a wide selection of handcrafted notebooks, journals, and fountain pens, each exuding old-world charm and elegance. Prices at Antica Cartoleria vary depending on the item's quality and craftsmanship, with many affordable options available for stationery enthusiasts. The shop is open from 10:30 AM to 7:30 PM, Monday to Saturday, and can be reached on foot or by public transportation, with the Lanza metro station nearby.

Milan's artisanal craft shops and souvenir boutiques offer a delightful shopping experience for visitors eager to explore the city's cultural heritage. Whether you're seeking handmade ceramics, traditional masks, or artisanal stationery, these establishments showcase the talent and creativity of local artisans. With convenient opening hours and easy accessibility via public transportation, exploring Milan's artisanal crafts and souvenirs is a must-do for anyone looking to take home a piece of the city's vibrant cultural scene.

9.4 Specialty Food Shops and Markets

Milan, a city renowned for its culinary delights and gastronomic traditions, is home to a plethora of specialty food shops and markets offering a treasure trove of gourmet products. From artisanal cheeses to freshly baked pastries, these establishments showcase the best of Italian cuisine, delighting the taste buds of locals and visitors alike. Here, we delve into six distinctive specialty food shops and markets in Milan, each offering its own unique array of culinary delights and shopping experience.

Peck: Located in the heart of Milan's bustling city center, Peck is a legendary gourmet food emporium that has been tantalizing taste buds since 1883. This iconic institution boasts an impressive selection of high-quality delicacies, including fine cheeses, cured meats, truffles, and freshly prepared dishes. Visitors can explore the sprawling store and indulge in tastings of Italian specialties, accompanied by expert guidance from the knowledgeable staff. Prices at Peck vary depending on the product's rarity and quality, with some gourmet items commanding premium prices. The store is open from 9:00 AM to 8:00 PM, Monday to Saturday, and is conveniently located near the Duomo metro station.

Eataly Milano Smeraldo: Situated in the vibrant Piazza XXV Aprile, Eataly Milano Smeraldo is a food lover's paradise, offering a diverse selection of Italian delicacies under one roof. This expansive market-cum-food hall features artisanal products from across Italy, including pasta, olive oil, wine, and freshly baked bread. Visitors can dine in one of the onsite restaurants or explore the various food counters offering made-to-order dishes and gourmet treats. Prices at Eataly Milano Smeraldo range from affordable to premium, catering to a wide range of budgets. The market is open from 9:00 AM to 11:00 PM, Monday to Sunday, and can be easily accessed by tram or metro.

Mercato Metropolitano: Nestled in Milan's up-and-coming Porta Romana district, Mercato Metropolitano is a sprawling food market that celebrates the joys of sustainable eating and artisanal craftsmanship. Here, visitors can browse stalls brimming with organic produce, local cheeses, freshly baked goods, and international delicacies. The market also hosts cooking workshops, food festivals, and live music events, providing a vibrant and immersive experience for food enthusiasts. Prices at Mercato Metropolitano vary depending on the vendor and product, with many affordable options available for budget-conscious shoppers. The market is open from 9:00 AM to midnight, Monday to Sunday, and can be reached by tram or metro.

Via Paolo Sarpi: Known as Milan's Chinatown, Via Paolo Sarpi is a bustling street lined with specialty food shops and ethnic markets offering a taste of Asia in the heart of the city. Visitors can explore a diverse array of Chinese, Japanese, and Korean delicacies, including fresh seafood, exotic spices, and authentic street food. Prices along Via Paolo Sarpi are generally affordable, with many vendors offering competitive prices for imported goods and Asian ingredients. The street market is open throughout the day, with individual shop hours varying, making it an ideal destination for food lovers looking to explore Milan's multicultural culinary scene. Via Paolo Sarpi can be easily reached by tram or metro, with several stations serving the area.

Antica Latteria San Marco: Located in Milan's charming Brera district, Antica Latteria San Marco is a historic dairy shop dating back to the late 19th century. This family-owned establishment specializes in artisanal cheeses, fresh dairy products, and homemade specialties, including creamy burrata, tangy gorgonzola, and fragrant ricotta. Visitors can sample a variety of cheeses and purchase their favorites to enjoy later or as gifts for friends and family. Prices at Antica Latteria San Marco are reasonable, reflecting the quality and authenticity of the products. The shop is open from 8:00 AM to 8:00 PM, Monday to Saturday, and is conveniently located near the Moscova metro station.

Mercato Comunale di Via Fauche: Tucked away in Milan's residential Bovisa neighborhood, Mercato Comunale di Via Fauche is a hidden gem for foodies seeking fresh produce and local specialties. This vibrant market features a mix of vendors selling seasonal fruits and vegetables, artisanal cheeses, cured meats, and freshly baked bread. Visitors can shop like a local and immerse themselves in the lively atmosphere of the market, engaging with vendors and sampling regional delicacies. Prices at Mercato Comunale di Via Fauche are affordable, making it an ideal destination for budget-conscious shoppers. The market is open from 7:00 AM to 2:00 PM, Tuesday to Sunday, and can be reached by tram or bus.

Milan's specialty food shops and markets offer a culinary journey through Italy's rich gastronomic landscape, from gourmet delicacies to everyday staples. Whether you're exploring the historic halls of Peck or sampling street food in Chinatown, these establishments offer a sensory delight and a window into the vibrant food culture of the city.With convenient opening hours and easy accessibility via public transportation, exploring Milan's culinary delights is a must-do for any visitor looking to savor the flavors of Italy.

9.5 Shopping Malls and Department Stores

Milan, Italy's fashion capital, boasts a vibrant retail scene with a plethora of shopping malls and department stores catering to every taste and budget. From luxury boutiques to international brands, these establishments offer a diverse array of goods and products, making Milan a shopper's paradise. Here, we'll delve into six of the city's most prominent shopping destinations, each offering its own unique shopping experience and attractions.

Galleria Vittorio Emanuele II: Located in the heart of Milan, Galleria Vittorio Emanuele II is one of the world's oldest shopping malls and a symbol of the city's architectural and cultural heritage. This elegant arcade, named after the first king of Italy, is renowned for its stunning glass dome and ornate interiors. Here, visitors can shop at luxury boutiques such as Prada, Gucci, and Louis Vuitton, as well as dine at upscale cafes and restaurants. Prices at Galleria Vittorio Emanuele II can be high due to the exclusive nature of the brands, but the experience of shopping in this historic setting is worth the splurge. The mall is open from 9:00 AM to 10:00 PM, Monday to Sunday, and can be easily accessed from the Duomo metro station.

La Rinascente: Situated in Piazza del Duomo, La Rinascente is Milan's premier department store, providing a carefully selected range of fashion, beauty, home goods, and gourmet food items. Spread across eight floors, this iconic landmark features both international brands and Italian designers, catering to a diverse clientele. Visitors can shop for luxury clothing, cosmetics, accessories, and homeware, as well as enjoy panoramic views of the city from the top-floor terrace. Prices at La Rinascente vary depending on the brand and product category, with options available for every budget. The store typically opens from 9:30 AM to 9:00 PM, Monday to Sunday, and is conveniently located near the Duomo metro station.

Il Centro: Located on the outskirts of Milan in the municipality of Arese, Il Centro is one of Europe's largest shopping malls, spanning over 92,000 square meters. This modern complex features over 200 shops, including fashion retailers, electronics stores, and home furnishing outlets. Visitors can explore a wide range of brands, from high-street favorites like Zara and H&M to luxury labels such as Versace and Armani. Il Centro also offers dining options, entertainment facilities, and ample parking, making it a convenient destination for a day of shopping and leisure. Prices at the mall vary depending on the brand and product category, with discounts often available during sales periods. Il Centro is open from 10:00 AM to 9:00 PM, Monday to Sunday, and can be reached by car or public transportation.

CityLife Shopping District: Situated in the futuristic CityLife complex, CityLife ShoppingDistrict is a modern retail destination that merges shopping, dining, and entertainment within a stylish setting. This upscale mall features a curated selection of luxury and premium brands, including fashion boutiques, home decor stores, and gourmet food outlets. Visitors can browse the latest collections from international designers like Valentino, Saint Laurent, and Fendi, as well as enjoy culinary delights at upscale restaurants and cafes. Prices at CityLife Shopping District tend to be on the higher end due to the exclusive nature of the brands. The mall is open from 10:00 AM to 9:00 PM, Monday to Sunday, and is conveniently located near the Tre Torri metro station.

Centro Commerciale Fiordaliso: Situated in the southern suburb of Rozzano, Centro Commerciale Fiordaliso is one of Milan's largest shopping centers, offering a wide range of retail, dining, and entertainment options. This family-friendly mall features over 130 stores, including fashion retailers, electronics outlets, and specialty shops. Visitors can shop for everything from clothing and accessories to home goods and electronics, with brands ranging from affordable to high-end. Centro Commerciale Fiordaliso also boasts a multiplex cinema, indoor playground, and food court, making it a popular destination for shoppers of all ages. Prices at the mall vary depending on the brand and product category, with plenty of options available for budget-conscious shoppers. The mall typically opens from 9:00 AM to 9:00 PM, Monday to Sunday, and can be reached by car or public transportation.

Euroma2: Located just outside of Milan in the municipality of Rome, Euroma2 is one of Italy's largest shopping centers, offering a diverse array of retail, dining, and entertainment options. This modern complex features over 230 stores, including international fashion brands, electronics outlets, and specialty shops. Visitors can shop for everything from clothing and accessories to home goods and sporting equipment, with options available for every budget. Euroma2 also boasts a multiplex cinema, indoor ice skating rink, and gourmet food court, making it a popular destination for shoppers and families alike. Prices at the mall vary depending on the brand and product category, with discounts often available during sales periods. Euroma2 is open from 10:00 AM to 10:00 PM, Monday to Sunday, and can be reached by car or public transportation.

CHAPTER 10
DAY TRIPS AND EXCURSIONS

10.1 Lake Como: Scenic Beauty and Villas

Situated amidst the stunning landscapes of northern Italy, Lake Como is celebrated for its awe-inspiring views, quaint villages, and ancient villas. While well-known spots like Bellagio and Varenna often capture attention, there are numerous hidden treasures awaiting exploration by adventurous travelers in search of a more secluded experience. Here, we unveil conic gems on Lake Como that offer scenic beauty and showcase the grandeur of the region's historic villas.

Villa del Balbianello: Tucked away on the western shore of Lake Como near the village of Lenno, Villa del Balbianello is a true hidden gem. This stunning villa, perched atop a wooded promontory, offers breathtaking views of the lake and surrounding mountains. Visitors can explore the meticulously landscaped gardens, adorned with exotic plants and towering cypress trees, before venturing inside the villa to admire its opulent interiors and priceless art collection. The villa is open to the public for guided tours from March to November, with tickets priced at around €10-€15 per person. To reach Villa del Balbianello from Milan, travelers can take a train to Como and then a ferry to Lenno, followed by a short walk to the villa.

Villa Monastero: Located in the charming village of Varenna on the eastern shore of Lake Como, Villa Monastero is a hidden gem that exudes tranquility and charm. Originally established as a Cistercian convent dating back to the 12th century, the villa was subsequently transformed into a private residence and now serves as a cultural and educational center. Visitors can wander through the lush botanical gardens, featuring a diverse array of plant species from around the world, and explore the villa's elegant rooms adorned with period furnishings and historical artifacts. Entrance to Villa Monastero is around €10-€15 per person, with guided tours available. To get to Varenna from Milan, travelers can take a train to Varenna-Esino station, followed by a short walk to the villa.

Villa Carlotta: Situated in the village of Tremezzo on the western shore of Lake Como, Villa Carlotta is a magnificent neoclassical villa surrounded by lush gardens and towering trees. Built in the late 17th century, the villa boasts a rich history and houses a remarkable collection of art and sculptures, including works by Canova and Hayez. Guests have the opportunity to meander through the villa's lavish interiors, embellished with frescoes and authentic period furnishings, prior to leisurely exploring the vast botanical gardens, which feature exotic plants, romantic pathways, and scenic lake views. Entrance to Villa Carlotta is around €10-€15 per person, with guided tours available. To reach Tremezzo from Milan, travelers can take a train to Como and then a ferry to Tremezzo, followed by a short walk to the villa.

Villa Pliniana: Located in the village of Torno on the southeastern shore of Lake Como, Villa Pliniana is a hidden gem steeped in history and legend. Built in the 16th century, the villa is famous for its natural spring, known as the Fonte Pliniana, which is said to have inspired the writings of Pliny the Elder. Visitors can marvel at the villa's elegant architecture and lush gardens, which overlook the tranquil waters of the lake. While the villa itself is privately owned and not open to the public, the surrounding area offers scenic walking trails and panoramic viewpoints for visitors to enjoy. To reach Torno from Milan, travelers can take a train to Como and then a bus or taxi to Torno, followed by a short walk to the villa.

Villa Melzi: Situated in the village of Bellagio on the tip of the Bellagio Peninsula, Villa Melzi is a hidden gem that epitomizes the beauty and elegance of Lake Como. Built in the early 19th century, the villa is surrounded by enchanting gardens, featuring exotic plants, tranquil ponds, and statuesque monuments. Visitors can explore the villa's ornate rooms, adorned with neoclassical furnishings and historic artifacts, before strolling through the expansive gardens and enjoying panoramic views of the lake and mountains. Entrance to Villa Melzi is around €6-€10 per person, with guided tours available. To reach Bellagio from Milan, travelers can take a train to Como and then a ferry to Bellagio, followed by a short walk to the villa.

Villa Erba: Located in the town of Cernobbio on the western shore of Lake Como, Villa Erba is a hidden gem that showcases the region's rich cultural heritage and natural beauty. Originally built in the 19th century as a private residence, the villa is now used as a conference and exhibition center, hosting a variety of cultural events and art exhibitions throughout the year. Visitors can explore the villa's elegant interiors, featuring frescoes, marble columns, and period furnishings, before wandering through the manicured gardens and enjoying panoramic views of the lake. While the villa itself is not always open to the public, the surrounding area offers scenic walking paths and picturesque vistas for visitors to enjoy. To reach Cernobbio from Milan, travelers can take a train to Como and then a bus or taxi to Cernobbio, followed by a short walk to the villa.

Lake Como offers a captivating glimpse into the region's scenic beauty and rich history. From historic villas steeped in legend to tranquil gardens overlooking the lake, these hidden gems provide a unique and immersive experience for visitors seeking to explore beyond the beaten path. With convenient transportation options from Milan and affordable entrance fees, Lake Como's iconic treasures are within easy reach for travelers looking to escape the hustle and bustle of the city and immerse themselves in the serenity of the Italian lakeside.

10.2 Bergamo: Medieval Town and Venetian Walls

Nestled in the foothills of the Italian Alps, Bergamo is a hidden gem that often gets overshadowed by its more famous neighbors. However, this medieval town boasts a rich history, charming cobblestone streets, and impressive Venetian walls, making it a must-visit destination for travelers seeking an off-the-beaten-path experience. Here, we uncover six iconic gems in Bergamo that offer a glimpse into its medieval past and architectural wonders.

Città Alta (Upper Town): Perched atop a hill overlooking the modern city, Città Alta is the historic heart of Bergamo and a UNESCO World Heritage Site. Visitors can step back in time as they wander through narrow cobblestone streets, past medieval palaces, churches, and charming piazzas. Highlights include the stunning Piazza Vecchia, the imposing Palazzo della Ragione, and the magnificent Basilica di Santa Maria Maggiore, adorned with beautiful frescoes and marble columns. To reach Città Alta from Milan, travelers can take a train from Milano Centrale to Bergamo station, followed by a short bus ride or funicular to the upper town.

Venetian Walls: Surrounding Città Alta, the Venetian Walls are a remarkable example of military architecture and one of Bergamo's most iconic landmarks. Built in the 16th century to defend against invaders, the walls stretch for over six kilometers and feature impressive ramparts, bastions, and gates. Visitors can stroll along the panoramic walkways atop the walls, enjoying breathtaking views of the surrounding countryside and city below. To access the Venetian Walls, travelers can simply walk from Città Alta's main square, Piazza Vecchia, to one of the several entry points along the fortifications.

San Vigilio Hill: Rising above Città Alta, San Vigilio Hill offers panoramic views of Bergamo and the surrounding Lombardy region. Visitors can hike or take a scenic funicular ride to the top, where they'll find the ruins of an ancient castle and a charming hilltop village. The hill is also home to the Torre del Gombito, a medieval tower offering 360-degree views of the city. To reach San Vigilio Hill, travelers can walk or take a bus from Città Alta's main square, Piazza Vecchia, to the base of the hill, where they can catch the funicular to the summit.

Basilica di Santa Maria Maggiore: Located in the heart of Città Alta, the Basilica di Santa Maria Maggiore is one of Bergamo's most important religious sites and a masterpiece of Renaissance architecture. Visitors can marvel at the basilica's ornate facade, adorned with intricate carvings and statues, before stepping inside to admire its stunning interior. Highlights include the magnificent main altar, the intricate wooden choir stalls, and the exquisite frescoes adorning the walls and ceiling. The basilica is open to visitors daily, with guided tours available for a nominal fee.

Accademia Carrara: Situated at the foot of Città Alta, the Accademia Carrara is an art museum housed in a beautiful neoclassical building. The museum's collection includes masterpieces by Italian Renaissance artists such as Botticelli, Raphael, and Titian, as well as works by Dutch and Flemish masters. Visitors can wander through the museum's galleries, admiring its impressive collection of paintings, sculptures, and decorative arts. The Accademia Carrara is open to the public from Tuesday to Sunday, with admission prices ranging from €8 to €12.

Bergamo Cathedral (Duomo di Bergamo): Located in the heart of Città Alta, the Bergamo Cathedral is a stunning example of Romanesque and Baroque architecture. Visitors can marvel at the cathedral's ornate facade, featuring intricate carvings and sculptures, before stepping inside to admire its richly decorated interior. Highlights include the stunning marble altar, the elaborate wooden choir stalls, and the impressive frescoes adorning the walls and ceiling. The cathedral is open to visitors daily, with guided tours available for a small fee.

Bergamo's off-the-beaten-path discoveries offer a captivating glimpse into its medieval past and architectural wonders. From the charming streets of Città Alta to the panoramic views atop San Vigilio Hill, visitors can immerse themselves in the town's rich history and cultural heritage. With convenient transportation options from Milan and affordable admission prices, Bergamo's iconic gems are within easy reach for travelers looking to explore beyond the beaten path and discover the hidden treasures of northern Italy.

10.3 Verona: Romantic City of Romeo and Juliet

Nestled in the heart of the Veneto region, Verona is a city steeped in history, culture, and romance. While best known as the setting for Shakespeare's tragic love story of Romeo and Juliet, Verona offers much more beyond its iconic landmarks. From hidden piazzas to charming neighborhoods, here are six off-the-beaten-path discoveries in Verona that promise to enchant visitors seeking a deeper immersion into the city's rich heritage.

Exploring the Historic District: Verona's historic district, with its maze of cobblestone streets and medieval architecture, is a treasure trove waiting to be discovered. Visitors can wander through hidden alleys and picturesque squares, stumbling upon hidden gems such as the Piazza delle Erbe, a lively market square enveloped by vibrant buildings and significant historical landmarks. Here, vendors sell fresh produce, souvenirs, and local delicacies, creating a vibrant atmosphere that captures the essence of Verona's daily life.

Castelvecchio Museum: Tucked away near the Adige River, Castelvecchio Museum is a lesser-known gem that houses an impressive collection of medieval and Renaissance art. Housed within a historic fortress built in the 14th century, the museum's collection includes paintings, sculptures, and decorative arts from the Veronese school, as well as artifacts from the city's rich history. Visitors can explore the museum's galleries and enjoy panoramic views of the city from the castle's ramparts. Admission to Castelvecchio Museum is around €6-€8 per person, with discounted rates for students and seniors.

San Zeno Maggiore: Situated in the quiet San Zeno neighborhood, San Zeno Maggiore is one of Verona's most important churches and a masterpiece of Romanesque architecture. Dedicated to Saint Zeno, the patron saint of Verona, the church features a stunning facade adorned with intricate carvings and sculptures. Inside, visitors can admire the beautiful frescoes, marble columns, and ornate altar, as well as the famous bronze doors depicting biblical scenes. San Zeno Maggiore is open to the public daily, with guided tours available for a small fee.

Giardino Giusti: Tucked away behind high walls near the city center, Giardino Giusti is a hidden oasis of tranquility and beauty. Dating back to the 16th century, the garden features manicured lawns, winding pathways, and ancient statues, providing a tranquil retreat from the hustle and bustle of urban life. Visitors can explore the garden's terraces and enjoy panoramic views of Verona from the top, as well as admire the elegant Renaissance-style villa that overlooks the grounds. Entrance to Giardino Giusti is around €6-€8 per person, with discounts for children and seniors.

Teatro Romano: Located on the banks of the Adige River, Teatro Romano is a well-preserved Roman amphitheater dating back to the 1st century. While not as famous as the Arena di Verona, this smaller amphitheater offers a fascinating glimpse into Verona's ancient past. Visitors can explore the ruins of the theater and imagine the spectacles that once took place within its walls, including gladiator fights and theatrical performances. Entrance to Teatro Romano is around €4-€6 per person, with discounts for students and seniors.

Ponte Pietra: Spanning the Adige River near the historic center, Ponte Pietra is one of Verona's oldest and most picturesque bridges. Dating back to Roman times, the bridge features a series of arches and elegant balustrades, offering stunning views of the river and surrounding landscape. Visitors can stroll across the bridge and admire its architectural beauty, as well as enjoy panoramic views of Verona's skyline from the riverbanks below. Ponte Pietra is a popular spot for photography and romantic walks, especially at sunset when the bridge is bathed in golden light.

Verona's off-the-beaten-path discoveries offer a captivating glimpse into the city's rich history, culture, and romance. From hidden churches and museums to tranquil gardens and ancient ruins, these lesser-known gems promise to enchant visitors seeking a deeper immersion into the city's timeless allure. With convenient transportation options from Milan and affordable admission prices, Verona's iconic treasures are within easy reach for travelers looking to explore beyond the beaten path and uncover the hidden gems of this romantic city.

10.4 Pavia: Historic University Town

Pavia is a charming and historic university town that often flies under the radar of tourists. However, this hidden gem offers a wealth of cultural treasures, picturesque landscapes, and architectural wonders waiting to be discovered. Here, we unveil six off-the-beaten-path day trips and excursions in Pavia that promise to captivate visitors seeking a deeper immersion into the city's rich heritage.

The Certosa di Pavia: Just a short distance from the city center lies the Certosa di Pavia, a stunning monastery and architectural masterpiece. Founded in the 14th century, the Certosa is renowned for its intricate Gothic facade, elegant cloisters, and richly decorated chapels. Visitors can explore the monastery's ornate interiors, adorned with frescoes, marble sculptures, and golden altars, as well as wander through the peaceful gardens and courtyards. The Certosa di Pavia is open to the public daily, with admission prices ranging from €10-€15 per person. To reach the Certosa from Milan, travelers can take a train from Milano Centrale to Pavia station, followed by a short bus or taxi ride to the monastery.

The Ponte Coperto: Spanning the Ticino River in the heart of Pavia, the Ponte Coperto is a picturesque stone bridge that dates back to the 14th century. Also known as the Covered Bridge, this iconic landmark is adorned with charming arches and elegant statues, offering stunning views of the river and surrounding countryside. Visitors can stroll across the bridge and admire its architectural beauty, as well as enjoy a leisurely riverside walk along the Ticino's scenic banks. The Ponte Coperto is accessible on foot from Pavia's city center and makes for a delightful afternoon excursion.

The Visconti Castle: Dominating the skyline of Pavia's historic center, the Visconti Castle is a medieval fortress that once served as the residence of the powerful Visconti family. Built in the 14th century, the castle features imposing towers, crenellated walls, and a majestic central courtyard. Visitors can explore the castle's interior, which houses a museum showcasing artifacts from Pavia's history, including medieval weapons, armor, and artwork. The Visconti Castle is open to the public daily, with admission prices ranging from €5-€8 per person. To reach the castle, travelers can walk from Pavia's city center or take a short bus or taxi ride.

The Ticino Natural Park: For nature enthusiasts, the Ticino Natural Park offers a peaceful retreat from the hustle and bustle of city life. Located just outside of Pavia, this vast nature reserve is home to lush forests, meandering rivers, and diverse wildlife. Visitors can explore the park's network of hiking trails, which wind through scenic landscapes and offer opportunities for birdwatching, picnicking, and photography. The Ticino Natural Park is accessible by car or public transportation from Pavia, with several entrance points and parking facilities available.

The Basilica di San Michele Maggiore: Situated in Pavia's historic center, the Basilica di San Michele Maggiore is a magnificent example of Lombard Romanesque architecture. Dating back to the 11th century, the basilica features a striking facade adorned with intricate carvings, as well as a majestic interior with soaring arches, ornate columns, and beautiful frescoes. Visitors can admire the basilica's architectural details and historical significance, as well as attend religious services and cultural events held within its sacred walls. The Basilica di San Michele Maggiore is open to the public daily, with free admission for visitors.

The University of Pavia Botanical Garden: Founded in the 16th century, the University of Pavia Botanical Garden is one of the oldest in Europe and a hidden gem waiting to be discovered. Located near the city center, the garden is home to a diverse collection of plant species from around the world, as well as historic greenhouses, water features, and sculptures. Visitors can wander through the garden's tranquil pathways, admire rare and exotic plants, and learn about the importance of biodiversity and conservation. The University of Pavia Botanical Garden is open to the public on weekdays, with free admission for visitors.

Pavia's day trips and excursions offer a captivating glimpse into the city's rich history, culture, and natural beauty. From medieval monasteries and historic bridges to lush parks and botanical gardens, these hidden gems promise to enchant visitors seeking a deeper immersion into Pavia's timeless allure. With convenient transportation options from Milan and affordable admission prices, Pavia's iconic treasures are within easy reach for travelers looking to explore beyond the beaten path and uncover the hidden gems of this historic university town.

10.5 Turin: Baroque Architecture and Museums

Turin, the capital of Italy's Piedmont region, is a city steeped in history, culture, and architectural splendor. While it's known for its grand boulevards, historic cafes, and royal palaces, Turin also boasts several off-the-beaten-path gems waiting to be discovered. From hidden churches to lesser-known museums, here are iconic destinations for day trips and excursions in Turin that offer a deeper immersion into the city's Baroque architecture and rich cultural heritage.

Basilica di Superga: Perched atop a hill overlooking Turin, the Basilica di Superga is a magnificent Baroque church with panoramic views of the city and surrounding Alps. Built in the 18th century to commemorate a victory over the French, the basilica is renowned for its majestic dome, ornate interior, and impressive collection of artworks.

Visitors can explore the church's elegant chapels, admire the stunning frescoes adorning the ceilings, and enjoy sweeping views of Turin from the observation deck. To reach the Basilica di Superga from Milan, travelers can take a train from Milano Centrale to Turin's Porta Susa station, followed by a short bus or taxi ride to the hilltop.

Museum of the Risorgimento: Located in Turin's historic center, the Museum of the Risorgimento is a hidden gem that chronicles Italy's struggle for independence and unification in the 19th century. Housed within the Palazzo Carignano, a stunning Baroque palace, the museum features a rich collection of artifacts, documents, and multimedia exhibits that bring this pivotal period of Italian history to life. Visitors can learn about the key events, personalities, and movements that shaped the Risorgimento, from the Napoleonic Wars to the founding of the Kingdom of Italy. The Museum of the Risorgimento is open to the public daily, with admission prices ranging from €5-€10 per person.

Palazzo Madama: Situated in the heart of Turin's historic center, Palazzo Madama is a UNESCO World Heritage Site and one of the city's most iconic landmarks. Built in the 13th century as a fortress, the palace was later transformed into a royal residence and now houses the Turin City Museum of Ancient Art. Visitors can explore the palace's elegant rooms, adorned with frescoes, stuccoes, and period furnishings, as well as admire its impressive collection of medieval and Renaissance artworks. Palazzo Madama is open to the public daily, with admission prices ranging from €5-€10 per person.

Basilica di Maria Ausiliatrice: Located in the Valdocco neighborhood of Turin, the Basilica di Maria Ausiliatrice is a hidden gem that showcases the city's rich religious heritage. Built in the late 19th century in the Neo-Gothic style, the basilica is renowned for its striking facade, towering spires, and magnificent stained glass windows. Visitors can explore the church's interior, which features intricate marble altars, ornate sculptures, and beautiful mosaics, as well as attend Mass or participate in guided tours.

The Basilica di Maria Ausiliatrice is open to the public daily, with free admission for visitors.

Museum of Oriental Art: Tucked away in Turin's Crocetta neighborhood, the Museum of Oriental Art is a lesser-known gem that offers a fascinating glimpse into the art and culture of Asia. Housed within a beautiful Art Nouveau villa, the museum's collection includes ancient artifacts, textiles, ceramics, and sculptures from China, Japan, India, and other Asian countries. Visitors can explore the museum's galleries, which are arranged thematically and feature rotating exhibitions highlighting different aspects of Asian art and civilization. The Museum of Oriental Art is open to the public daily, with admission prices ranging from €5-€8 per person.

Villa della Regina: Nestled on the outskirts of Turin, Villa della Regina is a hidden gem that showcases the city's aristocratic heritage and Baroque architecture. Built in the 17th century as a summer residence for the royal family, the villa boasts lush gardens, elegant fountains, and panoramic views of the surrounding countryside. Visitors can explore the villa's opulent interiors, which are adorned with frescoes, tapestries, and period furnishings, as well as wander through the landscaped grounds and enjoy a leisurely stroll along the tree-lined pathways. Villa della Regina is open to the public daily, with guided tours available for a small fee.

Turin's day trips and excursions offer a captivating glimpse into the city's Baroque architecture, rich cultural heritage, and hidden treasures. From majestic basilicas and historic palaces to lesser-known museums and gardens, these iconic destinations promise to enchant visitors seeking a deeper immersion into Turin's timeless allure. With convenient transportation options from Milan and affordable admission prices, Turin's off-the-beaten-path gems are within easy reach for travelers looking to explore beyond the city center and uncover the hidden gems of this historic Italian city.

CHAPTER 11
ENTERTAINMENT AND NIGHTLIFE

11.1 Restaurants: Gastronomic Experiences

Click the link or Scan QR Code with a device to view a comprehensive map of various Restaurants in Milan – https://shorturl.at/qtEPS

Milan, the vibrant fashion and cultural capital of Italy, is also renowned for its richculinary scene, providing a wide array of dining choices spanning from classic trattorias to Michelin-starred restaurants. Here, we delve into restaurants in Milan that promise to provide unforgettable gastronomic experiences.

Trattoria Milanese - A Taste of Tradition

Located in the heart of Milan's historic center, Trattoria Milanese embodies the essence of traditional Lombard cuisine. Situated near the iconic Duomo di Milano, this cozy trattoria welcomes diners with its warm ambiance and rustic décor. Here, visitors can savor classic Milanese dishes such as ossobuco, risotto alla milanese, and cotoletta alla milanese, paired with a selection of regional wines. Open for lunch and dinner, Trattoria Milanese offers a glimpse into Milan's culinary heritage, with dishes prepared using time-honored recipes passed down through generations.

Ratanà - Contemporary Italian Cuisine

Nestled in the trendy Isola district, Ratanà offers a modern twist on traditional Italian fare. This Michelin Bib Gourmand restaurant prides itself on using locally sourced ingredients to create innovative and flavorful dishes that celebrate Italy's culinary heritage. From handmade pasta to creative seafood preparations, Ratanà's menu showcases the diversity of Italian cuisine while highlighting the flavors of Lombardy. The restaurant's stylish interior and attentive service add to the overall dining experience, making it a favorite among locals and visitors alike. Ratanà is open for lunch and dinner, with extended hours on weekends to accommodate late-night diners.

10 Corso Como Café - Fashionable Dining

Situated within the iconic 10 Corso Como concept store, 10 Corso Como Café offers a chic and stylish dining experience in the heart of Milan's fashion district. This trendy café features a sleek design, with minimalist décor and floor-to-ceiling windows overlooking the bustling courtyard. Visitors can enjoy a light lunch or afternoon aperitivo while browsing the latest fashion collections and art exhibitions. The menu at 10 Corso Como Café includes an array of salads, sandwiches, and artisanal pastries, as well as a selection of cocktails and specialty coffees. Open from morning until late evening, the café is the perfect spot for a fashionable meal or a leisurely break between shopping sprees.

Peck - Culinary Excellence

For a gourmet dining experience steeped in tradition and elegance, look no further than Peck. Located near Milan's historic Galleria Vittorio Emanuele II, this iconic gourmet food emporium and restaurant has been delighting diners for over 130 years. Peck's restaurant offers a refined menu inspired by Italian culinary traditions, with an emphasis on seasonal ingredients and meticulous preparation. Diners can indulge in exquisite dishes such as homemade ravioli, grilled meats, and decadent desserts, accompanied by an extensive wine list featuring the finest Italian vintages. Peck is open for lunch and dinner, with reservations recommended for dinner service.

Drogheria Milanese - A Hidden Gem

Tucked away in the charming Brera district, Drogheria Milanese is a hidden gem known for its authentic Milanese cuisine and cozy atmosphere. Housed in a historic building dating back to the 18th century,this family-operated trattoria radiates an old-world allure, featuring exposed brick walls, wooden beams, and vintage decorations. Drogheria Milanese's menu features classic Lombard dishes made with locally sourced ingredients, including creamy risottos, hearty stews, and traditional desserts. Diners can also sample a variety of regional wines and liqueurs, handpicked by the restaurant's knowledgeable staff. Open for lunch and dinner, Drogheria Milanese offers a taste of Milan's culinary heritage in a charming and intimate setting.

Al Pont de Ferr - Michelin-Starred Excellence

For a truly exceptional dining experience, Al Pont de Ferr offers Michelin-starred cuisine in a picturesque setting along the Naviglio Grande canal. This elegant restaurant combines innovative culinary techniques with the finest seasonal ingredients to create exquisite dishes that tantalize the palate. The menu at Al Pont de Ferr showcases the creativity and artistry of Chef Matteo Monti, with dishes that marry traditional Italian flavors with contemporary flair. Diners can choose from a variety of tasting menus, each highlighting different aspects of Italian cuisine, accompanied by an extensive wine list featuring rare and exclusive labels. Al Pont de Ferr is open for dinner, with reservations required due to its popularity among discerning diners. Milan's culinary scene presents a diverse range of dining experiences, from authentic trattorias to Michelin-starred restaurants, each providing a unique glimpse into Italy's rich gastronomic heritage. Whether seeking classic Milanese fare or contemporary cuisine, visitors to Milan are sure to find a restaurant that satisfies their cravings and leaves a lasting impression.

11.2 Bars and Pubs: Local Hangouts

Click the link or Scan QR Code with a device to view a comprehensive map of various Bars and Pubs in Milan – https://shorturl.at/gzJRY

In Milan, the vibrant nightlife scene is just as much a part of the city's culture as its fashion and design. Amidst the bustling streets and elegant piazzas, you'll find a plethora of bars and pubs where locals gather to unwind, socialize, and enjoy a taste of Milanese hospitality. Let's discuss the diverse establishments that offer unique experiences for visitors looking to immerse themselves in Milan's local hangouts.

Nottingham Forest

Located in the heart of Milan's Brera district, Nottingham Forest is a renowned cocktail bar that has gained international acclaim for its innovative drinks and avant-garde atmosphere. Inspired by the adventures of Robin Hood, the bar's whimsical decor features Sherwood Forest-themed furnishings, while the menu boasts an extensive selection of cocktails crafted with precision and creativity. From molecular mixology to classic concoctions with a twist, each drink is a work of art designed to tantalize the taste buds. Nottingham Forest is open from Tuesday to Sunday, with opening hours typically from 6:00 PM until late.

Bar Basso

Situated in the bustling Porta Venezia neighborhood, Bar Basso is a historic institution that has been serving up signature cocktails since 1967. Famous for inventing the iconic Negroni Sbagliato, the bar exudes retro charm with its vintage decor and cozy ambiance. Alongside classic cocktails, Bar Basso offers a selection of traditional Italian aperitivi, including spritzes, vermouths, and artisanal liqueurs. Visitors can enjoy complimentary snacks with their drinks, such as olives, cheese, and crostini. Bar Basso is open daily from late morning until late evening, making it a popular spot for both locals and tourists alike.

Mag Cafè

Nestled in the vibrant Navigli district, Mag Cafè is a cozy hideaway known for its laid-back atmosphere and eclectic decor. The bar's vintage furnishings and quirky artwork create a retro-chic vibe, while the extensive cocktail menu features both classic concoctions and innovative creations. Visitors can sip on expertly crafted drinks while listening to live music or soaking up the atmosphere on the outdoor terrace overlooking the canal. Mag Cafè also offers a selection of light bites and appetizers to complement the drinks. The bar is open daily from late afternoon until late evening, with extended hours on weekends.

Rita

Located in the trendy Isola district, Rita is a stylish cocktail bar with a modern and minimalist aesthetic. The bar's sleek design and intimate atmosphere make it a popular spot for locals seeking a sophisticated yet relaxed setting to enjoy drinks with friends. Rita's menu focuses on quality ingredients and innovative flavor combinations, with an emphasis on seasonal and locally sourced produce. In addition to cocktails, the bar offers a curated selection of wines, beers, and artisanal spirits. Rita is open from Tuesday to Sunday, with opening hours typically from early evening until late.

Lelephant

Situated in the dynamic Porta Genova district, Lelephant is a hip and eclectic bar that draws inspiration from global travel and urban culture. The bar's eclectic decor features vintage furnishings, graffiti art, and exotic artifacts, creating a vibrant and eclectic ambiance. Lelephant's menu showcases a diverse selection of cocktails, with an emphasis on bold flavors and creative presentations. Visitors can also sample a variety of craft beers, wines, and spirits from around the world. Lelephant hosts regular events and DJ sets, making it a lively destination for nightlife enthusiasts. The bar is open daily from early evening until late, with extended hours on weekends.

Barrio

Located in the multicultural Porta Ticinese district, Barrio is a lively neighborhood bar that celebrates diversity and community. The bar's vibrant decor and welcoming atmosphere reflect the eclectic mix of cultures and influences found in the surrounding area. Barrio's menu features a range of craft cocktails, artisanal beers, and Latin-inspired drinks, as well as a selection of tapas and small plates to share. Visitors can enjoy live music, DJ sets, and cultural events throughout the week, creating a vibrant and inclusive space for socializing and relaxation. Barrio is open daily from late afternoon until late evening, with extended hours on weekends.

Milan's local hangouts offer a diverse array of experiences for visitors looking to immerse themselves in the city's vibrant nightlife scene. From historic institutions to hip and eclectic bars, each establishment has its own unique charm and character, reflecting the diverse culture and creativity of Milan. Whether you're sipping on a classic Negroni or sampling innovative cocktails crafted with precision and flair, these six bars and pubs provide the perfect opportunity to mingle with locals, soak up the atmosphere, and enjoy a taste of Milanese hospitality.

11.3 Nightclubs and Live Music Venues

Milan offers a diverse array of options for those seeking to dance the night away or groove to the beats of talented musicians. Here, I'll introduce you to six of the city's most exciting and memorable nightlife destinations that are sure to leave you wanting more.

Plastic

Located in the heart of Milan's vibrant Navigli district, Plastic is a legendary nightclub that has been a fixture of the city's nightlife scene for over 35 years. With its retro-chic decor, pulsating beats, and electric atmosphere, Plastic offers an unforgettable clubbing experience for partygoers of all ages. The club hosts some of the hottest DJs and international acts, drawing crowds from around the world. Entry prices vary depending on the night and any special events, but expect to pay around €20-€30 for admission. Plastic is open on Fridays and Saturdays from midnight until late, ensuring that the party never stops.

Just Cavalli

For those seeking a taste of luxury and glamour, look no further than Just Cavalli, a lavish nightclub located in the trendy Porta Nuova district. Owned by fashion designer Roberto Cavalli, this opulent venue exudes sophistication with its chic decor, VIP tables, and state-of-the-art sound system. Guests can dance the night away to the beats of top DJs while sipping on expertly crafted cocktails and rubbing shoulders with Milan's elite crowd. Entry prices can be steep, particularly for special events and guest appearances, so be prepared to shell out anywhere from €30-€50 for admission. Just Cavalli is open on Thursdays, Fridays, and Saturdays from midnight until the early hours of the morning.

Tunnel Club

Tucked away beneath the railway arches near Milan's Porta Garibaldi station, Tunnel Club is a hidden gem that promises an unforgettable underground clubbing experience. With its industrial-chic decor, immersive light shows, and cutting-edge electronic music, Tunnel Club attracts a diverse crowd of music lovers and party enthusiasts. The club hosts regular themed nights and live performances by both local and international artists, ensuring that every visit is a unique and memorable experience. Entry prices typically range from €15-€25, with discounts available for early birds and student nights. Tunnel Club is open on Fridays and Saturdays from midnight until dawn, offering a sanctuary for night owls and dance enthusiasts alike.

Blue Note Milano

For a more refined and intimate nightlife experience, look no further than Blue Note Milano, a world-renowned jazz club located in the heart of Milan's historic city center. With its intimate setting, superb acoustics, and stellar lineup of jazz musicians, Blue Note Milano offers an unparalleled live music experience for aficionados and novices alike. Guests can enjoy performances by jazz legends and emerging talents while savoring delicious cocktails and gourmet cuisine. Entry prices vary depending on the artist and performance, but expect to pay around €30-€50 for admission. Blue Note Milano is open from Tuesday to Sunday, with multiple shows each evening starting at 9:00 PM.

Alcatraz

Situated in the bustling Isola district, Alcatraz is a sprawling nightclub and live music venue housed in a former industrial space. With its eclectic mix of music genres, energetic atmosphere, and state-of-the-art sound system, Alcatraz offers something for everyone, from live concerts and DJ sets to themed parties and cultural events. The club's diverse lineup attracts a diverse crowd of music lovers and partygoers, ensuring that every night is a unique and unforgettable experience. Entry prices vary depending on the event and artist, but expect to pay around €15-€30 for admission. Alcatraz is open on select nights of the week, with doors typically opening at 10:00 PM.

Bobino Club

Located in the vibrant Porta Romana district, Bobino Club is a beloved institution that has been entertaining Milan's nightlife enthusiasts for over 50 years. With its retro-inspired decor, eclectic music selection, and laid-back vibe, Bobino Club offers a welcoming and inclusive atmosphere for guests of all ages. The club hosts a variety of themed nights, including retro parties, karaoke nights, and live music performances, ensuring that there's always something fun and exciting happening. Entry prices are affordable, with admission typically ranging from €10-€20 depending on the night and any special events. Bobino Club is open on Fridays and Saturdays from midnight until late, inviting visitors to dance, laugh, and create lasting memories in the heart of Milan.

Milan's nightlife scene offers a diverse array of experiences for travelers seeking to dance, groove, and immerse themselves in the city's vibrant energy. From legendary nightclubs to intimate live music venues, each establishment has its own unique charm and character, ensuring that there's something for everyone to enjoy. So, why not step out of your comfort zone and experience the magic of Milan's nightlife for yourself? With its pulsating beats, electric atmosphere, and unforgettable memories waiting to be made, Milan is sure to leave a lasting impression on your soul.

11.4 Cultural Events and Performances

Milan is a city teeming with cultural events and performances that showcase its rich history, artistic heritage, and diverse community. From world-class exhibitions to mesmerizing performances, here are six cultural experiences that will captivate your senses and leave you longing to explore the cultural heart of Milan.

La Scala Opera House

No visit to Milan is complete without experiencing the magic of La Scala Opera House, one of the most prestigious and renowned opera houses in the world. Located in the heart of the city, La Scala has been captivating audiences with its breathtaking productions since 1778. From classic operas by Verdi and Puccini to ballet performances and symphony concerts, each show at La Scala is a feast for the senses, showcasing the unparalleled talent of the world's finest musicians, singers, and dancers. Ticket prices vary depending on the performance and seating, with options ranging from affordable gallery seats to luxurious box seats. Regardless of where you sit, attending a performance at La Scala is a once-in-a-lifetime experience that will leave you spellbound.

Teatro alla Scala Museum

For those who want to delve deeper into the history and heritage of La Scala, a visit to the Teatro alla Scala Museum is a must. Housed within the opera house itself, the museum offers a fascinating journey through the centuries, with exhibits that trace the evolution of opera, ballet, and theater. Visitors can explore rare manuscripts, costumes, and props from past productions, as well as learn about the lives and careers of the artists who have graced the stage of La Scala. The museum also features interactive displays and multimedia installations that bring the history of opera to life. Entry to the Teatro alla Scala Museum is affordable, with tickets priced around €10-€15 per person.

Milan Fashion Week

As the fashion capital of Italy, Milan is home to one of the most prestigious events in the fashion industry: Milan Fashion Week. Held twice a year in February/March and September/October, Fashion Week attracts designers, models, and fashion enthusiasts from around the world to showcase the latest trends and collections. From glamorous runway shows to exclusive parties and pop-up events, Fashion Week offers a glimpse into the cutting-edge world of haute couture and luxury fashion. While tickets to runway shows are typically reserved for industry insiders, there are plenty of public events and exhibitions throughout the city that allow visitors to experience the excitement and glamour of Fashion Week firsthand.

Brera Design District

For design enthusiasts, a visit to the Brera Design District is an opportunity to immerse yourself in Milan's thriving design scene. Located in the historic Brera neighborhood, the district comes alive during Milan Design Week, an annual event held in April that showcases the latest innovations in furniture, lighting, and interior design. Visitors can explore exhibitions, installations, and showrooms hosted by leading design brands and emerging designers, as well as attend lectures, workshops, and networking events. The Brera Design District also boasts a vibrant arts and culture scene, with galleries, museums, and cultural institutions showcasing contemporary art and design year-round.

Milan Film Festival

Film buffs and cinephiles won't want to miss the Milan Film Festival, a yearly occasion that honors independent cinema and up-and-coming filmmakers from various corners of the globe. Held in various venues throughout the city, the festival features a diverse lineup of feature films, documentaries, shorts, and experimental works, as well as special screenings, Q&A sessions, and panel discussions with filmmakers and industry professionals. Whether you're a fan of arthouse films, international cinema, or cutting-edge documentaries, the Milan Film Festival offers something for everyone to enjoy. Ticket prices vary depending on the screening and venue, with options for single tickets, festival passes, and VIP packages available.

Milan International Theatre Festival

For theater lovers, the Milan International Theatre Festival is a showcase of world-class performances and groundbreaking productions that push the boundaries of traditional theater. Held annually in May, the festival brings together theater companies, directors, and actors from around the globe to present a diverse program of plays, experimental theater, dance performances, and multimedia installations. From avant-garde dramas to immersive theatrical experiences, the Milan International Theatre Festival offers a unique opportunity to engage with contemporary theater and explore new forms of artistic expression. Ticket prices vary depending on the performance and venue, with options for single tickets, festival passes, and student discounts available.

Milan's cultural events and performances offer a captivating glimpse into the city's rich artistic heritage and creative spirit. From the grandeur of La Scala Opera House to the cutting-edge innovations of Milan Fashion Week, each experience is a testament to Milan's status as a global hub of culture and creativity. So why not immerse yourself in the cultural delights of Milan and discover the magic that awaits in this dynamic and vibrant city?

11.5 Safety Tips for Enjoying Milan's Nightlife

As a seasoned traveler and author who values firsthand experience, I understand the importance of staying safe while exploring the vibrant nightlife of Milan. While the city offers a wealth of exciting experiences and cultural delights after dark, it's essential to take precautions to ensure your well-being and enjoyment. Below are crucial safety pointers to bear in mind while enjoying Milan's vibrant nightlife scene.

Stay Aware of Your Surroundings

One of the most important safety tips for enjoying nightlife in Milan, or any city for that matter, is to stay aware of your surroundings at all times. Whether you're wandering through bustling streets or dancing the night away in a crowded club, it's crucial to remain vigilant and alert to any potential risks or dangers. Keep an eye on your belongings, avoid dark or isolated areas, and trust your instincts if you feel uncomfortable in any situation. By staying aware and attentive, you can minimize the risk of encountering any unwanted incidents while enjoying Milan's nightlife.

Travel in Groups

Another essential safety tip for enjoying nightlife in Milan is to travel in groups whenever possible. Whether you're exploring the city's bars, clubs, or cultural events, having friends or companions by your side can provide an added layer of security and support.

Stick together, look out for one another, and establish a plan for staying connected throughout the night. Not only does traveling in groups enhance your safety, but it also allows you to share memorable experiences and create lasting memories with your companions.

Plan Your Transportation

When venturing out into Milan's nightlife, it's essential to plan your transportation ahead of time to ensure a safe journey home. Whether you're relying on public transportation, rideshare services, or taxis, familiarize yourself with the routes, schedules, and options available for getting around the city after dark. Avoid walking alone late at night, especially in unfamiliar or poorly lit areas, and consider arranging a designated driver or alternative transportation if you plan to indulge in alcoholic beverages. By planning your transportation in advance, you can enjoy your night out in Milan with peace of mind and confidence.

Drink Responsibly

While it's tempting to indulge in the delicious cocktails and beverages offered at Milan's bars and clubs, it's essential to drink responsibly to ensure your safety and well-being. Pace yourself, alternate alcoholic drinks with water, and know your limits to avoid overindulgence and its associated risks. Be mindful of your surroundings and watch out for any signs of intoxication in yourself or others. If you feel unwell or impaired, seek assistance from friends, staff, or emergency services to ensure you get home safely. By drinking responsibly, you can enjoy the vibrant nightlife of Milan without compromising your safety or health.

Trust Your Instincts

One of the most powerful tools for staying safe while enjoying nightlife in Milan is to trust your instincts and intuition. If something doesn't feel right or if you sense danger or discomfort in any situation, don't hesitate to remove yourself from the situation and seek assistance if needed. Whether it's avoiding a crowded or rowdy establishment, declining invitations from strangers, or opting to leave a situation that feels unsafe, trust your gut instincts and prioritize your well-being above all else. By listening to your inner voice and acting on your instincts, you can navigate Milan's nightlife with confidence and peace of mind.

Stay Connected

Lastly, staying connected with friends, family, or trusted contacts is essential for ensuring your safety while enjoying nightlife in Milan. Keep your phone charged and accessible, share your location with trusted contacts, and establish a communication plan for checking in throughout the night. Let someone know your plans, whereabouts, and expected return time, and don't hesitate to reach out for help or support if needed. By staying connected and maintaining open lines of communication, you can enjoy your night out in Milan knowing that help is just a call or message away if you need it. While Milan's nightlife offers a wealth of exciting experiences and cultural delights, it's essential to prioritize safety and well-being while exploring the city after dark. By staying aware of your surroundings, traveling in groups, planning your transportation, drinking responsibly, trusting your instincts, and staying connected, you can enjoy the vibrant nightlife of Milan with confidence, peace of mind, and unforgettable memories. So why not embrace the magic of Milan's nightlife and immerse yourself in the city's vibrant energy and cultural richness? With these essential safety tips in mind, you can enjoy all that Milan has to offer while staying safe, secure, and ready for adventure.

CONCLUSION AND INSIDER TIPS FOR VISITORS

As we draw to a close in our exploration of Milan, the vibrant city of art, fashion, and culture, it's essential to leave you with some insider tips and final thoughts to ensure your visit is nothing short of extraordinary. With a wealth of firsthand experience and knowledge at our disposal, let's delve into some key insights and recommendations that will enhance your journey and leave you with unforgettable memories of Milan.

Embrace the Milanese Way of Life

One of the most rewarding aspects of visiting Milan is immersing yourself in the city's unique lifestyle and culture. Embrace the Milanese way of life by indulging in leisurely strolls along the elegant boulevards, savoring delicious Italian cuisine at local trattorias and cafes, and experiencing the city's vibrant nightlife scene. Take the time to engage with locals, learn about their traditions and customs, and embrace the spirit of la dolce vita that permeates every corner of Milan.

Discover Hidden Gems Off the Beaten Path

While iconic landmarks like the Duomo and La Scala Opera House are must-see attractions, don't overlook the hidden gems and lesser-known corners of Milan. Venture off the beaten path to discover charming neighborhoods, historic churches, and hidden courtyards that offer glimpses into the city's rich history and architectural heritage. From the tranquil gardens of Villa Necchi Campiglio to the artistic enclave of the Brera district, Milan is full of surprises waiting to be discovered.

Plan Your Visit Around Cultural Events and Festivals

To truly experience the vibrancy of Milan, consider planning your visit around one of the city's many cultural events and festivals. From Milan Fashion Week to the Salone del Mobile furniture fair, there's always something exciting happening in the city. Check the event calendar and plan your itinerary to coincide with concerts, exhibitions, and performances that align with your interests. Attending these events not only provides unique cultural experiences but also allows you to immerse yourself in the dynamic energy of Milan.

Explore Beyond the City Limits

While Milan offers endless opportunities for exploration within the city limits, don't hesitate to venture beyond its borders to discover the beauty of the surrounding Lombardy region.Embark on a day excursion to the scenic Lake Como or venture into the historic towns of Bergamo and Pavia.Alternatively, head to the nearby wine regions of Franciacorta or Valtellina for a taste of Italy's finest wines. Exploring the diverse landscapes and charming towns surrounding Milan offers a refreshing perspective and enriches your travel experience.

Utilize Public Transportation

Navigating Milan's bustling streets and narrow alleyways can be daunting, but the city's efficient public transportation system makes getting around a breeze. Utilize the extensive network of buses, trams, and metro lines to explore the city with ease. Consider purchasing a MilanoCard for unlimited access to public transportation and discounts on attractions, or opt for a bike rental to explore the city on two wheels. By utilizing public transportation, you'll save time, money, and energy while maximizing your time in Milan.

Embrace the Spirit of Adventure

Above all, embrace the spirit of adventure and curiosity that fuels your travels. Allow yourself to get lost in the labyrinthine streets of Milan, stumble upon hidden gems, and forge unforgettable memories along the way. Don't be afraid to try new foods, strike up conversations with locals, and step outside your comfort zone. Milan is a city brimming with possibility and promise, and by embracing the unknown, you'll uncover treasures beyond your wildest imagination.

In conclusion, Milan is a city that captivates the hearts and minds of travelers from around the world with its timeless beauty, rich history, and boundless creativity. As you embark on your journey to Milan and beyond, remember to embrace the Milanese lifestyle, discover hidden gems, plan your visit around cultural events, explore beyond the city limits, utilize public transportation, and above all, embrace the spirit of adventure. By following these insider tips and recommendations, you'll unlock the true essence of Milan and create memories that will last a lifetime. So pack your bags, embark on your journey, and let Milan's magic unfold before your eyes.

Buon viaggio!!!

MILAN TRAVEL PLANNER

NAME:
_____

DEPARTURE DATE:
_____

RETURN DATE:
_____

MY PACKING LIST

- _____
- _____
- _____
- _____
- _____
- _____
- _____
- _____
- _____
- _____

MY TRAVEL BUDGET

- _____
- _____
- _____
- _____
- _____
- _____
- _____
- _____
- _____
- _____
- _____
- _____
- _____
- _____
- _____
- _____
- _____
- _____
- _____

A-7 DAY TRAVEL ITINERARIES PLANNING

DAY 1:

DAY 2:

DAY 3:

DAY 4:

DAY 5:

DAY 6:

DAY 7

MUST-DO THINGS IN MILAN

- _____
- _____
- _____
- _____
- _____
- _____
- _____
- _____
- _____
- _____
- _____
- _____
- _____
- _____
- _____

MUST-TRY FOOD IN MILAN

-
-
-
-
-
-
-
-
-
-
-
-
-
-
-

LIST OF TOURIST SITES & HIDDEN GEMS TO VISIT IN MILAN

-
-
-
-
-
-
-
-
-
-
-
-
-
-

SHARE YOUR MILAN TRAVEL EXPERIENCE

Printed in Great Britain
by Amazon